A Practical Guide to Relief from Sanctions Post-Mitchell and Denton

AF722182

A Practical Guide to Relief from Sanctions Post-Mitchell and Denton

Peter Causton MA (Cantab),
Solicitor Advocate and Barrister at Law,
Deputy District Judge, International Online Mediator,
Civil and Commercial Mediator (ProMediate (UK) Limited)

Law Brief Publishing

© Peter Causton

All rights reserved. No part of this publication may be reproduced, stored in a retrieval system, or transmitted, in any form or by any means, electronic, mechanical, photocopying, recording or otherwise, without the prior permission of the publisher.

Excerpts from judgments and statutes are Crown copyright. Any Crown Copyright material is reproduced with the permission of the Controller of OPSI and the Queen's Printer for Scotland. Some quotations may be licensed under the terms of the Open Government Licence (http://www.nationalarchives.gov.uk/doc/open-government-licence/version/3).

Cover image © iStockphoto.com/mw_listing

The information in this book was believed to be correct at the time of writing. All content is for information purposes only and is not intended as legal advice. No liability is accepted by either the publisher or author for any errors or omissions (whether negligent or not) that it may contain. Professional advice should always be obtained before applying any information to particular circumstances.

Published 2018 by Law Brief Publishing, an imprint of Law Brief Publishing Ltd
30 The Parks
Minehead
Somerset
TA24 8BT

www.lawbriefpublishing.com

Paperback: 978-1-911035-44-2

This book is dedicated to my partner, Nichola Evans, who has been so supportive and to all the advocates in the North West who have had to put up with the vagaries of my judgments as a deputy district judge.

PREFACE

The author of this book had in mind as the audience for this book any lawyers and advocates needing guidance on bringing and defending applications for relief from sanctions.

The law on relief from sanctions is likely to continue to evolve but this first edition of the book states the law as it is on 1st October 2018.

Peter Causton
October 2018

CONTENTS

CHAPTER ONE
INTRODUCTION

One of the most difficult situations that a party can face is having their case struck out for failure to comply with a procedural error, whether their own fault or their Solicitors'. Put simply, it can be the end of the litigation road, even if the limitation period has not expired. That is because starting new proceedings can amount to an abuse of process. Compliance with rules, orders and Practice directions has become an objective of the Court, which has now almost become a third party in litigation.

That is why parties need to know how to apply for relief from sanction and how to defend such applications, as sanctions can deliver a knockout blow to an opponent.

This guide seeks to assist in the situation where you check a file and find that the Court deadline for an action has passed, such as applying to lift a stay, serving a disclosure statement, or costs budget, and a sanction will or may be imposed.

Here are some examples of situations when relief may be needed from start to finish in litigation. This list is not exhaustive, as we will explain:

- Costs budgets
- Pleadings – dates for service of Defence, Reply, Requests for Further Information
- Setting aside judgment
- Unless Orders
- Stays where they have expired
- Directions Questionnaires – failure to serve

- Disclosure
- Witness statements
- Expert evidence
- Non-payment of Court fees – Sanctions for non-payment of Court fees – CPR Part 3.7

Since the Jackson reforms were introduced in 2013, and the Civil Procedure Rules with their "overriding objective" and case management powers, practitioners have had to grapple with the Courts' new emphasis upon compliance with rules, orders and practice directions and the efficient use of the Courts' resources. Used to being able to agree directions and extensions of time, lawyers have often found themselves unwittingly in default and draconian sanctions applied. Practitioners have not seen a concurrent increase in the efficiency of the Courts and it often seems ironic that a punitive sanction can be imposed for missing a deadline when the Courts are very slow at dealing with cases and can cancel or change Court hearing times and venues without consulting the parties. The individual circumstances of the Court and its capacity does not appear to be a relevant factor at present and parties seldom try to argue that moving a trial date will not impact upon the Court's resources or other litigants. There is almost a presumption that moving a trial date will inconvenience the Court, when in fact it may not have that effect as the Courts are under-resourced.

The majority of reported relief from sanction cases have concerned personal injury claims, which is perhaps unsurprising when they are dealt with in bulk and systems sometimes break down. This may decrease following the personal injury reforms as the objective is to reduce the number of low value personal injury claims that are issued. Following the case of Denton and the three-stage test for relief from sanctions, there is now more leeway, and parties are not meant to try to obtain a tactical advantage from another party's mistakes, but nonetheless applications for relief from sanction have increased and there have been many decisions in the Court of Appeal. While each case turns on its own merits, we aim in this Guide to provide some guidance to parties to assist them in bringing and defending such applications.

We do not consider that the developments in the law have now ceased and we are sure that more decisions will be handed down on the issue in the coming years. In particular, the Courts have not necessarily got the balance right between the breach and the sanction applied, as illustrated in the Mitchell case. Sanctions can be completely disproportionate and unjust. We anticipate further decisions on the three-stage test and what constitutes a "good reason", "seriousness" and what factors should be considered in "all the circumstances of the case", as well as the over-arching principle of the right to a fair trial, which parties are often deprived of in relief from sanctions cases. Meanwhile, lawyers need to tighten up their procedures and try to avoid sanctions being applied in the first place, which will lead to fewer applications and happier clients. No lawyer wants to have to tell their client that no compensation or remedy will be available thanks to a missed deadline.

As a deputy district judge, apart from dealing with Stage III /disposal hearings, holiday sickness claims, possession hearings, etc, we often see applications for relief from sanctions.

This gives me a useful insight into what works best when applying for relief and escaping what can be a tricky situation for litigators.

The Relief from Sanctions Rule

There is no better place to start than the rule itself and secondary rules:

The Relief from sanctions rule is set out in CPR 3.9:

> *3.9*
>
> *(1) On an application for relief from any sanction imposed for a failure to comply with any rule, practice direction or court order, the*

court will consider all the circumstances of the case, so as to enable it to deal justly with the application, including the need –

(a) for litigation to be conducted efficiently and at proportionate cost; and

(b) to enforce compliance with rules, practice directions and orders.

(2) An application for relief must be supported by evidence.

Note that it is important that any application is supported by evidence. The rule has to be understood in the context of rule 3.8:

<u>Sanctions have effect unless defaulting party obtains relief</u>

3.8

(1) *Where a party has failed to comply with a rule, practice direction or court order, any sanction for failure to comply imposed by the rule, practice direction or court order has effect* ***<u>unless the party in default applies for and obtains relief from the sanction.</u>***

(Rule 3.9 sets out the circumstances which the court will consider on an application to grant relief from a sanction)

It is important to note that you need to apply for relief where a sanction has been imposed, or *could be imposed,* for breach.

This means that even if the Order does not specify that the sanction has effect, it is still necessary to make an application. If in doubt, apply! The only situation where the rule does not apply is in relation to costs, as the rule sets out that:

(2) *Where the sanction is the payment of costs, the party in default may only obtain relief by appealing against the order for costs.*

It is possible to agree an extension for 28 days without Court approval, as long as this does not affect any hearing date:

> (3) *Where a rule, practice direction or court order –*
>
> *(a) requires a party to do something within a specified time, and*
>
> *(b) specifies the consequence of failure to comply,*
>
> *the time for doing the act in question may not be extended by agreement between the parties except as provided in paragraph (4).*
>
> (4) *In the circumstances referred to in paragraph (3) and unless the court orders otherwise, the time for doing the act in question may be extended by prior written agreement of the parties for up to a maximum of 28 days, provided always that any such extension does not put at risk any hearing date.*

This means that by PRIOR agreement, the parties can agree up to 28 days extension for any step where there is a sanction.

The Overriding Objective is also relevant:

> *The overriding objective*
>
> *1.1*
>
> *(1) These Rules are a new procedural code with the overriding objective of enabling the court to deal with cases justly and at proportionate cost.*
>
> *(2) Dealing with a case justly and at proportionate cost includes, so far as is practicable –*
>
> *(a) ensuring that the parties are on an equal footing;*
>
> *(b) saving expense;*

(c) dealing with the case in ways which are proportionate –

(i) to the amount of money involved;
(ii) to the importance of the case;
(iii) to the complexity of the issues; and
(iv) to the financial position of each party;

(d) ensuring that it is dealt with expeditiously and fairly;

(e) allotting to it an appropriate share of the court's resources, while taking into account the need to allot resources to other cases; and

(f) enforcing compliance with rules, practice directions and orders.

The overriding objective makes clear that the Court's resources and its time are no longer infinite. We all know that listing hearings is a difficult business as cases can settle on the day and so the Courts tend to over-list. Sometimes this results in hearings being ineffective through no fault of the parties, but nonetheless, Court time is now a valuable resource that needs to be considered. We would say that parties could assist with this by notifying the Court earlier when a case settles, rather than the day before the trial, but there is currently no sanction for settling a case and failing to inform the Court expeditiously.

The rules make clear that by the court has to apply the overriding objective:

1.2

The court must seek to give effect to the overriding objective when it –

(a) exercises any power given to it by the Rules; or

(b) interprets any rule subject to rules 76.2, 79.2 and 80.2, 82.2 and 88.2.

Moreover, it is a duty of the parties to help to promote the overriding objective:

1.3

The parties are required to help the court to further the overriding objective.

Court's duty to manage cases

1.4

(1) The court must further the overriding objective by actively managing cases.

(2) Active case management includes –

(a) encouraging the parties to co-operate with each other in the conduct of the proceedings;

(b) identifying the issues at an early stage;

(c) deciding promptly which issues need full investigation and trial and accordingly disposing summarily of the others;

(d) deciding the order in which issues are to be resolved;

(e) encouraging the parties to use an alternative dispute resolution(GL)procedure if the court considers that appropriate and facilitating the use of such procedure;

(f) helping the parties to settle the whole or part of the case;

(g) fixing timetables or otherwise controlling the progress of the case;

(h) considering whether the likely benefits of taking a particular step justify the cost of taking it;

(i) dealing with as many aspects of the case as it can on the same occasion;

(j) dealing with the case without the parties needing to attend at court;

(k) making use of technology; and

(l) giving directions to ensure that the trial of a case proceeds quickly and efficiently.

The Courts have general powers to rectify matters where there has been an error of procedure:

***3.10** Where there has been an error of procedure such as a failure to comply with a rule or practice direction –*

(a) the error does not invalidate any step taken in the proceedings unless the court so orders; and

(b) the court may make an order to remedy the error.

Such errors are not normally those for which relief is sought, but if an error has been made, that may assist in an application for relief. The Court has extensive powers to extend time and to control the litigation timetable. Moving the trial date has become sacrosanct, because justice delayed is justice denied and the Courts have targets for cases proceeding to trial. Recent MOJ statistics show that in the last quarter of 2017, there were 73,000 claims defended and 14,000 claims that had gone to trial in October to December 2017, up 3% and 1% respectively.

The average time taken for small claims to trial took 32.2 weeks and for multi/fast track claims 58.3 weeks, up 1.8 and 5.4 weeks on the same period in 2016 respectively. However, average time taken continues to be in line with range seen since 2011.

To deal with the issue of delay, the rules provide that an extension of time for 28 days can only be agreed if it does not affect a hearing date. This might also include an interlocutory hearing date and not just a trial.

Bear in mind that if the applicant is unrepresented and applies for relief, the Court is likely to be more indulgent towards them –

> *3.1A*
>
> *(1) This rule applies in any proceedings where at least one party is unrepresented.*
>
> *(2) When the court is exercising any powers of case management, it must have regard to the fact that at least one party is unrepresented.*

In practice, the Court will always be more open to a litigant in person who has fallen foul of a rule as they try to navigate around an unfamiliar system. This is particularly so in the small claims Court where often the unrepresented parties fail to disclose their documents and witness statements in good time before the hearing, but strict evidential rules do not apply. The judge in the small claims court is likely to allow a litigant in person to escape a sanction in such circumstances without making an application.

It will be interesting to see how sanctions will apply with the introduction of the new online Court system. No doubt there will continue to be failures by litigants to comply with the rules and applications may be dealt with electronically or on paper. New challenges are bound to be thrown up for the Courts to consider.

CHAPTER TWO
BACKGROUND HISTORY: FROM WOOLF TO JACKSON TO DYSON

Prior to the implementation of the Jackson reforms, it was considered that the courts had become too tolerant of parties' non-compliance with orders, rules and practice directions and the delays this non-compliance caused.

It was originally Lord Woolf who started the whole process of reform in his Access to Justice Report which heralded the introduction of the Civil Procedure rules. His report was revolutionary in scope and he shook up the litigation system which until then had trundled along slowly for many decades. I distinctly remember in pupillage attending the Master to argue that cases which had been issued years before should be struck out for "want of prosecution" as nothing had been done and litigants would routinely extend time limits for all steps in litigation. Something had to change.

Lord Woolf envisaged a New Landscape for the Civil justice which included the following features:

- Litigation will be avoided wherever possible
- Litigation will be less adversarial and more co-operative.
- Litigation will be less complex.
- The timescale of litigation will be shorter and more certain.
- The cost of litigation will be more affordable, more predictable, and more proportionate to the value and complexity of individual cases.

- Parties of limited financial means will be able to conduct litigation on a more equal footing

- There will be clear lines of judicial and administrative responsibility for the civil justice system.

- Judges will be deployed effectively so that they can manage litigation in accordance with the new rules and protocols

- The civil justice system will be responsive to the needs of litigants.

He considered that "the introduction of judicial case management is crucial to the changes which are necessary in our civil justice system. Ultimate responsibility for the control of litigation must move from the litigants and their legal advisers to the court...Experience in developing case management in other jurisdictions has indicated that not all cases require the same hands-on management but that a differential approach is needed. Research on existing systems has also shown the efficacy of timetabling. These developments show the way forward.

There are those who have misgivings about the need for my proposals and their ability to effect beneficial change. Concern has been expressed that my proposals for case management will undermine the adversarial nature of our civil justice system. The concerns are not justified. The responsibility of the parties and the legal profession for handling cases will remain. The legal profession will, however, be performing its traditional adversarial role in a managed environment governed by the courts and by the rules which will focus effort on the key issues rather than allowing every issue to be pursued regardless of expense and time, as at present.

It has also been suggested that judges are not well equipped to be managers. I do not see the active management of litigation as being outside a judge's function. It is an essential means of furthering what must be the objective of any procedural system, which is to deal with cases justly. Case management includes identifying the issues in the case; summarily disposing of some issues and deciding in which order other issues are to be resolved; fixing timetables for the parties to take particular steps in the case; and limiting disclosure and expert evidence. These are all judicial functions. They are extensions backwards in time of the role of the trial judge"

Lord Woolf recommended that sanctions be applied for failure to comply with orders and directions. He reported that:

> "*There are certain key management stages, or 'milestones', in a case which should be established at the outset and which it should not be possible to move except with the permission of the court. These stages would be the case management conference, the pre-trial review and the trial date. But apart from these key stages the parties would be able to agree changes to the timetable subject to the overriding power of the court to intervene if appropriate. Any such agreement to vary a timetable, and the reasons for it, must be sent to the court (and to the client). Any extension must be for a specific period and the parties should file a new timetable.*
>
> *Where one party seeks an extension of time to which the other does not agree, he may apply prospectively for an extension of time. If that time has passed he would have to apply to the court for relief from the sanction which would be imposed in the event of his non-compliance with the time limit. He would have to satisfy the court that he had complied with other directions and that there was a good reason why he was unable to comply with the direction in question. Save in exceptional circumstances he would also have to pay the other side's costs of the application immediately.*"

His concept is worthwhile repeating:

> "*There must of course be some limited right to apply for relief from a sanction. In my view the onus should be on the party in default to seek relief, not on the other party to apply to enforce the sanction. The application should be made before the date of expiry of the specific requirement. It is important that the conditions for relief should be set out clearly in the rules. I recommend, broadly following the test in*

Rastin v British Steel [1994] 1 WLR 732, that relief should not be granted unless the court is satisfied that the breach was not intentional, that there has been substantial compliance with other directions and that there is a good explanation. The court will need to consider whether the failure was due to the default of the client, whether the default had been or could be remedied within a reasonable period, whether the trial date, or next milestone date, could still be met if relief were granted, and whether granting relief would cause more prejudice to the respondent than refusal would to the applicant. The normal order in these cases will be for the costs of the application, as assessed by the court, to be paid immediately by the party at fault. In many cases the applicant's solicitor would have to pay the respondent's costs and would not be entitled to recover them from his client. Where relief is not applied for until after the relevant time has expired it will only be allowed in exceptional circumstances and the applicant would normally bear the costs. In considering whether there is prejudice the courts must be prepared to acknowledge that delay in itself is prejudicial to a party who is seeking a decision. The client should personally be sent any costs order made against him and be made aware of his right to apply for a wasted costs order against his solicitor. He should also be sent a copy of any order breach of which will lead to striking out, so he knows the directions of the court and the effect of non-compliance.

To a large extent the effectiveness of sanctions will revolve around judicial attitudes. There is no doubt that some judges at first instance, especially Masters and district judges, will need to develop a more robust approach to the task of managing cases and ensuring that their orders are not flouted. They must, in particular, be resistant to applications to extend a set timetable, save in exceptional circumstances. But these judges must also be supported both by the trial judge and by courts hearing appeals. Many people who commented also stressed the need for consistency between the trial judge and the judge who had imposed sanctions for earlier procedural breaches. If the fast track, in particular, is to work it will be necessary for the rules to make it clear that it will not normally be acceptable to overturn earlier procedural decisions unless there has been a material

> *and unforeseeable change of circumstances and it would not be possible to deal with the case fairly without doing so. So far as appeals are concerned, procedural decisions must not be overturned lightly but only when judges have misdirected themselves as to the facts or the law or made errors of principle. This is not simply a matter of limiting appeals. It goes to a change of culture, in which judges can make orders confident that parties will not feel that they can ignore orders or that they can escape unscathed by appealing."*

So, the relief from sanction rule was born.

He set the sanctions ball rolling. He said that in the new climate he was envisaging, sanctions should play their proper role, which is "prevention rather than punishment" Where a sanction had to be applied he recommended that it should be "fair, relevant and simple to administer and must not create additional costs or delay for the party not at fault".

His recommendations for the new rule were as follows:

(1) As part of a case-managed system, sanctions should be designed to prevent, rather than punish, non-compliance with rules and timetables.

(2) The rules themselves should specify what will happen where there has been a breach. All directions orders should include an automatic sanction for non-compliance.

(3) The court should intervene and impose sanctions on parties who conduct litigation in an unreasonable or oppressive manner even if they have not breached specific rules, orders or directions.

(4) The courts should make more use of their power to tax or assess the costs of an application and order them to be paid immediately.

(5) The onus should be on the party in default to seek relief from a sanction, not on the other party to apply to enforce the sanction.

(6) The power to make wasted costs orders should continue, but they should be reserved for clear cases and not allowed to develop into satellite litigation.

(7) The client should personally be sent any costs order made against him and be made aware of his right to apply for a wasted costs order against his solicitor. He should also be sent a copy of any order, breach of which will lead to striking out, so that he knows the directions of the court and the effect of non-compliance."

Generally speaking, these were the recommendations which were implemented, although orders are not always sent to the client, much as clients do not always, or often, attend case management hearings as was envisaged.

The inquiry by Woolf published its final report in 1996 and thereafter the proposals resulted in the Civil Procedure Act 1997 and the Civil Procedure Rules 1998 for the County court and High Court, supplemented by new practice directions and pre-action protocols.

Following on from Woolf, it was considered that complacency had set in again and costs were still disproportionate. Jackson's solution lay in more case and costs management by the judiciary. He said that:

> "*One of the points that was impressed upon me during the Costs Review was that judges should take a more robust approach to case management, to ensure that (realistic) timetables are observed and that costs are kept proportionate. Case management can and should be an effective tool for costs control.*
>
> *The courts, like the National Health Service, are a public service. Their function is to adjudicate disputes with available resources.*

> *Court users are only entitled to their fair share of court resources. At the moment judges, following the precept of CPR rules 3.8, 3.9 and 3.10 are far too indulgent to litigants in default. This causes not only delay but also unproductive waste of court resources in dealing with the effects of litigant failure to meet deadlines. It is only in truly extreme circumstances that the courts will strike out a party which is in default"*

Lord Justice Jackson was concerned with the "*damage this culture of delay and non-compliance [was] inflicting upon the civil justice system,*" and considered it needed to be addressed. The objective was to reduce costs through active case management by the Courts, which would no longer be inactive bystanders. This coincided with the economic problems in 2008, which ushered in an age of austerity. Even though parties pay for the privilege of litigating, the Court Service was increasingly seen as equivalent to the NHS, with abuse of its resources by users, no more so than by clinical negligence lawyers who were seen as a drain on the Courts' finances and increases in road traffic and other personal injury claims resulting in higher insurance premiums. One way of reducing cost was to push cases through a streamlined low cost Portal and strike them out for any serious breach of the Court timetable.

Jackson recommended redressing the balance between the Courts and litigants by emphasising the importance of complying with directions and by active case management, to include District Judges contacting parties directly to follow up orders, surely any litigant's worst nightmare.

"Securing compliance with case management directions is preferable to punishing non-compliance" he said. "I therefore recommend that, if and in so far as time allows, judges or clerks on their behalf should contact parties at appropriate stages in order to enquire what progress has been made in complying with orders and directions. I am told by practitioners who have litigated in the USA that nothing galvanises lawyers into action more effectively than an enquiry from the judge as to how they are getting on." Of course, that seldom happens as the

Court resources do not allow it, and District judges do not have "clerks" but this illustrates Jackson's radical approach to reform.

Jackson reported in 2009. Consequently, the Jackson reforms came in on 1 April 2013 and brought with it changes to the rules relating to applications for relief, with the new test requiring Judges to consider all the circumstances, so as to enable them to deal justly with applications.

The rule before the Reforms came into force set out the circumstances that the court must take into consideration on any such application, as follows:

> "*(1) On an application for relief from any sanction imposed for a failure to comply with any rule, practice direction or court order, the court will consider all the circumstances including -*
>
> *(a) the interests of the administration of justice;*
>
> *(b) whether the application for relief has been made promptly;*
>
> *(c) whether the failure to comply was intentional;*
>
> *(d) whether there is a good explanation for the failure;*
>
> *(e) the extent to which the party in default has complied with other rules, practice directions, court orders and any relevant pre-action protocol;*
>
> *(f) whether the failure to comply was caused by the party or his legal representative;*
>
> *(g) whether the trial date or the likely trial date can still be met if relief is granted;*
>
> *(h) the effect which the failure to comply had on each party; and*
>
> *(i) the effect which the granting of relief would have on each party.*"

These 9 factors were removed by The Civil Procedure (Amendment) Rules 2013 and CPR 3.9 with effect from 1 April 2013 became:

> *"(1) On an application for relief from any sanction imposed for a failure to comply with any rule, practice direction or court order, the court will consider all the circumstances of the case, so as to enable it to deal justly with the application, including the need –*
>
> *(a) for litigation to be conducted efficiently and at proportionate costs; and*
>
> *(b) to enforce compliance with rules, practice directions and orders."*

It was widely considered that the new rule's removal of the old rule's checklist would mean that parties would no longer be able to take advantage of the list of extenuating circumstances to assist them in an application for relief from sanctions.

Jackson also recommended that the Court of Appeal should be loathe to interfere with robust case management decisions by the lower Courts. He said that:

> *"It is a well-established principle that the Court of Appeal will be reluctant to interfere with case management decisions made by a first instance judge who has applied the correct principles, unless the decision is "so plainly wrong that it must be regarded as outside the generous ambit of discretion entrusted to the judge". Concern has recently been expressed that, despite this principle, the Court of Appeal is on occasions too ready to substitute its own views on case management issues. It would not be right for me to comment on the merits of individual decisions. Nevertheless, going forward, I do regard it as vital that the Court of Appeal supports first instance judges who make robust but fair case management decisions. If the costs of litigation generally are driven up by the Court of Appeal's efforts to protect a party against the consequences of his lawyers' mis-takes in an individual case, many other litigants will be denied access to justice altogether. Furthermore, whenever permission is granted to*

> *appeal against a case management decision, the timetable for the litigation in question is thrown into disarray."*

It was hoped that with the new more stringent test, and Lord Justice Jackson's final report in their minds, judges at all levels would take heed of the consequences non-compliance was having on the court system and take a far less tolerant approach to parties who departed from the rules. Until Denton, this was the message delivered to judges at Judicial Training courses, delivered to deputy district judges. We were told in no uncertain terms that we were to follow the direction of travel which was to be less tolerant of delay and breaches of the rules.

Post April 2013 and Mitchell

Unfortunately, immediately post 1 April 2013, what we actually saw was a very inconsistent application of the new test. Accordingly, when the first case relating to an application for relief from sanctions, Mitchell MP v New Group Newspapers Limited [2013] EWCA Civ 1537, came before it in November 2013 the Court of Appeal took the opportunity to lay down a no-nonsense approach when it came to relief from sanction.

Essentially, Mr Mitchell failed to serve a costs budget on time and the sanction was for all of his costs to be disallowed. He was limited to recovery of Court fees only. This seemed very unfair given that he had only been late in filing a costs budget. The punishment did not seem to fit the crime.

Costs budgeting had increasingly been seen as the answer to the problem of excessive costs, forcing solicitors to set out their likely costs in painstaking detail in advance of a costs and case management hearing, so that they could be gone through with a fine-tooth comb by the judge and approved or disallowed. The problem was that many judges had no interest or training in this exercise and so the costs budgeting exercise was unpredictable. Nonetheless the Mitchell case was designed to send a strong signal to lawyers that costs budgets were very important and must be filed on time.

The proceedings fell within the scope of the pre-Jackson defamation costs management pilot scheme. Mr Mitchell's solicitors breached the terms of the Practice Direction by failing to file and exchange a budget no later than seven days before the first costs management conference; and failing to engage in attempts to discuss budgets and budgetary assumptions.

Due to the breaches of Mr Mitchell's solicitors, the Master imposed the sanction under the costs management scheme by limiting Mr Mitchell's budget to Court fees only. As the Practice Direction provided that, when assessing costs on the standard basis, there is to be no departure from the last approved budget without good reason, this sanction effectively meant that Mr Mitchell would be unable to recover any legal costs from the Defendant in the event his claim was successful.

An application for relief from sanctions was therefore made on Mr Mitchell's behalf. The Master refused the Claimant's Application for relief and gave the following reasons:

> "*The explanations put forward by the claimant's solicitors are not unusual ones. Pressure of work, a small firm, unexpected delays with counsel and so on. These things happen, and I have no doubt they happened here. However, even before the advent of the new rules, the failure of solicitors was generally not treated as in itself a good excuse and I am afraid that however much I sympathise with the claimant's solicitors, such explanations carry even less weight in the post-Jackson environment.*"

What made the decision surprising is the fact that the Claimant's solicitor received notice of the CMC only four days before the costs budget was due. Although conceding that this was a point which "troubled" her, the learned Judge nevertheless continued:

> *"The parties were well aware that this was a case for which budgeting would be required from the start and that the mere fact that a date is set for a CMC is not supposed to be the starting gun for proper consideration of budgeting."*

The Court of Appeal determined that the sanction imposed by the Master was appropriate and that she had been entitled to use the new CPR 3.14 costs budgeting rule as guidance in this regard.

It was necessary for Mr Mitchell to apply for relief from sanctions.

The Court of Appeal considered that the breach was neither minor nor trivial and that no good reason had been provided to excuse the breach. In the circumstances, the Master could not be said to have misdirected herself.

It was submitted on Mr Mitchell's behalf that a more proportionate sanction would have been to allow 50% of his budget. It was accepted that such a sanction could be imposed but it was concluded that such a sanction would not often be appropriate as:

The merit of the rule is that it set out a simple default sanction. The expectation is that the sanction will usually apply unless (i) the breach is trivial or (ii) there is a good reason for it. It is true that the court has the power to grant relief, but the expectation is that, unless (i) or (ii) is satisfied, the two factors mentioned in the rule will usually trump other circumstances. If partial relief were to be encouraged, that would give rise to uncertainty and complexity and stimulate satellite litigation.
The effect is that Mr Mitchell's appeal was dismissed on all grounds. His costs budget remained as including Court fees only, and this was the limit of the costs which he was likely to be able to recover if his claim was successful. In the event he lost his case, so the decision was hypothetical in any event! He was found to have called the policemen "plebs."

The Court's overriding conclusion was that "relief from sanctions should be granted more sparingly than previously." Even though the requirement for 'promptness' had been removed from CPR 3.9 when it was redrafted, the Court of Appeal concluded that applications for relief should be made promptly.

The Mitchell case sent shock waves through the profession and resulted in an increase in professional indemnity insurance premiums. If a breach was non-trivial, it was incumbent on the defaulting party to provide a good reason for the default which would ordinarily be founded in circumstances outside of its control. Failure to comply with a deadline due to an oversight or due to pressure of work would not constitute a good reason.

Compliance with rules and practice directions was now seen as an end in itself and the use of valuable Court time became an important consideration.

This stringent approach attracted much negative comment as it was felt that the pendulum had swung too far the opposite way, penalising parties severely for minor breaches.

Over the past few years the courts have retreated from the excessively draconian approach seen immediately following the *Mitchell* decision and the sanction for filing a Costs budget late were altered This more measured approach was prompted in particular by the Court of Appeal's decision in *Denton* in July 2014 which "clarified" the *Mitchell* guidelines.

Denton Three-Stage Test

So through the following cases of ***Denton v TH White Ltd & Another, Decadent Vapours Ltd v Bevan & Others and Utilise TDS Ltd v Davies and Another [2014] EWCA Civ 906*** the Court of Appeal laid down more detailed guidance to assist lower courts when giving judgement on applications for relief. It also watered down the main rule to allow parties a "get out of jail card" – This guidance consisted of a three-stage test:

1. The court should identify and assess the seriousness or significance of the 'failure to comply with any rule, practice direction, or court order' which engages CPR 3.9(1);

2. The court should consider why the default occurred; - whether there was a "good reason"; and

3. The court should "evaluate all the circumstances of the case, so as to enable it to deal justly with the application including factors in CPR3.9(1)(a) and (b)" (which are set out above).

Parties were also not meant to try to take a tactical advantage from a breach of the rules. The profession breathed a collective sigh of relief, although the new interpretation of the rule still meant that there were high stakes to play for at any relief from sanction hearing. The Denton decision effectively brought back the list of extenuating circumstances which had been removed from the rule.

This case concerned the late service of witness statements in proceedings arising from the defendant's supply and installation of the claimants' milking parlour. Following exchanges of witness and expert evidence in 2012, a CMC took place in February 2013 and directions were given for the exchange of further expert evidence together with schedules of loss. The trial date was fixed for 13 January 2014. At the pre-trial review on 2 December 2013, the claimants/respondents served five witness statements. The hearing was adjourned. The claimants served another statement on 6 December and made an application for permission to rely on all six statements.

At the re-listed pre-trial review on 23 December 2013, the Judge gave the claimants permission to rely on the statements and vacated the trial date. The defendant appealed to the Court of Appeal on the ground that the judge failed to apply, or misapplied, Mitchell and erred in the exercise of his case management discretion.

In the case of Decadent Vapours Ltd v Bevan the claimant/appellant failed to comply with an unless order to file a pre-trial checklist and pay the required court fee by 4pm on 19 December 2013. The checklist was filed by email on the afternoon of 19 December but the cheque for the fee was only sent that day. It was never cashed but this did not come to light until the pre-trial review on 7 January 2014. The result of the claimant's failure to comply with the unless order meant that the claim stood as struck out. The fee was paid on 9 January 2014, almost immediately after the lost cheque was discovered.

The judge refused to grant the claimant relief from sanctions. He concluded that the claimant's solicitor made a conscious decision not to take steps to ensure that the fee was paid on time and knowing that the cheque would not arrive until at least the day after it was due.

In Utilise TDS Ltd v Davies the claimant/appellant failed to comply with an unless order requiring the parties to file costs budgets by 4pm on 11 October 2013, in default of which they could only claim court fees by way of costs if they were successful, as in Mitchell. The claimant missed the deadline by 45 minutes. The order also imposed a stay until 8 November and required the claimant to notify the court of the outcome of negotiations by 4pm on 15 November, but it was 13 days late in doing so. The District Judge dismissed the claimant's application for relief from the sanction for breaching the costs budget deadline, noting the lack of a good reason for the late filing and taking into account the claimant's failure to comply with the other deadline in the order. The claimant appealed.

The three appeals were heard by a panel consisting of the Master of the Rolls, who led the panel in Mitchell, Jackson LJ, whose recommendations led to the reforms and also Vos LJ.

The issues that were raised included:

- The loss of co-operation between parties to litigation. With the rise of "windfall" strike outs the approach following Mitchell meant it was no longer in the interest of litigators to ignore what are otherwise minimal breaches by the other side.

- The impact of the rule was too harsh: the failure by lower courts to look for any link between the breach and the nature of the sanction. All orders and timescales were being seen as unless orders, even those obligations in the CPR for which there was no sanction. The striking out actions or the debarring of evidence, which is often effectively the same thing, had become the only sanction being imposed, whether a breach is serious or minor.

- Given that the aim of the regime was to help with the efficiency of the administration of justice, there had been a massive growth in satellite litigation with huge costs being incurred in making relatively unnecessary applications.

- There was an inconsistency between courts such that lawyers were unable to give any clear advice about how to approach a failure to comply with the rules by their client, or the other side.

As a member of the Law Society's Civil Justice Committee, we had been involved in the implementation of the Jackson reforms and we assisted with the Law Society's intervention, as there was a lot of disquiet in the legal profession about the choking and straightjacketing effect of Mitchell on practitioners.

The Court of Appeal reviewed Rule 3.9 and made it clear that this decision should be all that any litigator needs to consider when trying to apply the rules. Mitchell, and the subsequent decisions, need not be referred to.

Lord Dyson MR and Vos LJ advocated a three-stage approach as follows:

The test of whether a breach is trivial became a test of whether a breach is serious or significant, recognising that the test can encompass the effect on other litigation. Although the fact of prior breaches will be relevant, they will be relevant only at stage 3.

The court should then consider whether there was good reason for the breach. If there is good reason, that will tend to justify granting relief from sanctions.

Only at this stage does the court need to consider the factors in Rule 3.9. Rule 3.9(1)(a) and (b) need to be considered and have a higher overall status than other reasons but the court must have regard to all the circumstances of the case. Previous breaches may therefore be a relevant factor, but only at this stage.

So, following Denton, it is clearer as to what practitioners need to do to pass the relief from sanctions test, which has been watered down to some extent, but is still not easy to do. The subsequent chapters will focus on cases that followed Denton and in which the test was applied in particular circumstances (as the Mitchell lines of authority are no longer strictly relevant) and then provide guidance as to how best to succeed in an application or defeat it.

CHAPTER THREE
RELIEF FROM COSTS BUDGETING SANCTIONS

One of the most controversial areas involving sanctions is the rules around costs budgeting. If those rules are ignored then the purpose of Jackson's reforms is arguably undermined as it is more difficult to control litigation costs. Some solicitors would describe costs budgeting as a waste of time, involving more time and cost for no discernible purpose. As a deputy District Judge we only received costs budgeting training in 2016. There is little drive towards consistency in decision making. One thing is sure, missing the deadline for a Costs budget is a high crime and misdemeanour worthy of sanction, as in the Mitchell case. In that case, the Costs budget was late but there was no real evidence that it adversely affected the other party or the Court to deserve being deprived of costs and limited to the Court fee, but it certainly sent a strong message to litigants – miss costs budgeting deadlines at your peril! Part of the problem in my view is that so few high court and Court of Appeal judges are solicitors with any experience of running a case load or managing costs from a practitioner's perspective. Barristers simply don't have enough understanding of what it is like to manage a case load. Until more solicitors are appointed as judges in the higher courts, decisions like Mitchell are likely to occur.

In considering an application for relief from sanctions for late filing of a Costs budget, the court will apply the three-stage test set out in *Denton*, namely: (i) the seriousness and significance of the breach; (ii) whether there was good reason for the breach; and (iii) all the circumstances of the case, giving particular weight to the two factors set out in CPR 3.9(1), ie (a) the need for litigation to be conducted efficiently and at proportionate cost and (b) the need to enforce compliance with rules, practice directions and orders.

Under CPR 3.14, any party which fails to file a costs budget despite being required to do so will be treated as having filed a budget comprising only the applicable court fees. That is a significant sanction because, when assessing costs on the standard basis, the court will not depart from a party's last approved or agreed budget unless there is good reason to do so. Being treated as having filed a budget limited only to court fees may therefore have a major impact on the costs a party can recover from its opponent if it is successful in the litigation.

In Andrew Mitchell v News Group Newspapers [2013] EWCA Civ 1537 the Court of Appeal confirmed that relief from sanctions would be very hard to come by unless a breach of a rule, order or practice direction could 'properly be regarded as trivial' or there was a 'good reason' for that breach.

Background

Following the Sun newspaper's reporting of an incident with a police man in Downing Street, Andrew Mitchell brought a defamation claim against the newspaper's publishers. It was alleged that he had called the police officers "plebs." The Claim was Issued in March 2013 and the proceedings were run under the PD51D Defamation case management pilot scheme. This required the parties to file costs budgets at least 7 days before the first CMC but did not specify a sanction for non-compliance.

Costs budgets formed part of the new costs management regime introduced to implement recommendations made in Lord Justice Jackson's Review of Civil Litigation Costs: Final Report. In most multi-track cases issued since 1 April 2013 each party, except litigants in person, must prepare a costs budget for the litigation. The budgets had to be filed and exchanged by the date specified in the Notice of Proposed Allocation or, if none, at least seven days before the date of the first case management conference (CPRr.3.13). Failure to do so carried an automatic sanction limiting that party's recoverable costs to court fees only, 'unless the court otherwise orders' (CPRr.3.14).

Mr Mitchell's solicitors filed their budget the day before the first CMC. The opponents had filed theirs in time. Without a specific sanction, the Master handling the CMC adopted the r.3.14 sanction by analogy, as it was the clearest indication of the appropriate sanction for failure to file a costs budget at least 7 days before the CMC. She gave leave to apply for relief from sanctions.

On the application for relief the Master considered the new overriding objective and the new CPR r.3.9 and refused relief. The estimated £500,000 costs would be irrecoverable. The Court of Appeal confirmed that this was the correct approach

Partially as a response to the Mitchell case, the costs budgeting rules were revised and came into force on the 6th April 2016. It does seem particularly unfair on the Claimant in such a case to be penalised by being unable to recover costs simply because their solicitor has made a mistake. Presumably professional indemnity insurers have to step in and become de facto ATE insurers in such a case.

The fact that there can be a considerable time gap between the court making an order and the order being sent out has meant, on some occasions, that the parties have had very little notice of the date of the first case management conference, yet the costs budget still has to be filed 21 days before the hearing. This is something about which all litigators should be aware.

New Dates for Filing of Costs Budgets

Note the dates for filing costs budgets:

> "*3.13.—(1) Unless the court otherwise orders, all parties except litigants in person must file and exchange budgets—*
>
> *(a) where the stated value of the claim on the claim form is less than £50,000, with their directions questionnaires; or*
>
> *(b) in any other case, not later than 21 days before the first case management conference.*

> *(2) In the event that a party files and exchanges a budget under paragraph (1), all other parties, not being litigants in person, must file an agreed budget discussion report no later than 7 days before the first case management conference.".*

The sanction for breach of the requirement to file a costs budget remains the same. Failure to file the budget in time means that the party in default has its costs budget limited to court fees (unless relief from sanction is obtained).

<u>New Requirements Where the Claim Is Valued Between £25,000 and £50,000</u>

There are changes to Practice Direction 3 – E Costs Management.

> *"(b) Parties must follow the Precedent H Guidance Note in all respects.*
>
> *(c) In cases where a party's budgeted costs do not exceed £25,000 or the value of the claim as stated on the claim form is less than £50,000, the parties must only use the first page of Precedent H.".*

The first of these requirements is as important as the second. The Precedent H Guidance Note must be followed "in all respects".

<u>The Budget Discussion Report</u>

There is a requirement to file a "budget discussion report". This must be filed no later than 7 days before the first case management conference.

> *"C. Budget discussion reports 6A.*
>
> *The budget discussion report required by rule 3.13(2) must set out—*
>
> *(a) those figures which are agreed for each phase;*

(b) those figures which are not agreed for each phase; and

(c) a brief summary of the grounds of dispute.

The parties are encouraged to use the Precedent R Budget Discussion Report annexed to this Practice Direction."

Subsequently there have been the following decisions dealing with Costs budgets and relief from sanction.

Murray v BAE Systems Plc 2016 – Costs Budget

The claimant filed its costs budget seven days late, meaning its entitlement to recover costs was limited to applicable court fees only. The claimant applied for relief from sanctions, but its application failed at first instance, so an appeal was filed.

The appeal was allowed. The judge hearing the appeal held that the first instance judge should not have rejected the suggestion that the consequences of the claimant's breach should be taken into account in categorising the nature of the breach. The breach had been caused by an isolated mistake made by the claimant's solicitor following a genuine breakdown in communications. The appeal judge therefore did not consider that the claimant's breach could fairly be categorised as "serious and significant" as the litigation could be conducted efficiently, at proportionate cost and without being adversely affected by the breach; that the application for relief had been made promptly; that there had been no previous breach in the proceedings; that the District Judge could have proceeded to assess the costs budget in any event; and that the claimant's solicitor's mistake was an isolated one and due to a genuine breakdown of communication.

The Appeal Judge found that consideration should have been given to where the breach lay on the scale of seriousness and significance and in this case considered m that it would fall towards the bottom of any applicable scale. Essentially, this decision took a much more sensible approach to the issue.

Jamadar -v- Bradford Teaching Hospitals NHS Trust [2016] EWCA Civ 1001

The failure to serve a costs budget was also considered in this case. The Court of Appeal upheld an order limiting recoverable costs to court fees where party failed to file costs budget

Lord Justice Jackson delivered the leading judgment dismissing an appeal against imposition of the sanction where a party failed to file a costs budget when required to do so, so that he was treated as having filed a budget limited to court fees.

Jackson LJ commented that other judges might have taken a more lenient view, but the judge had not erred in principle and it was a decision he was entitled to reach within the ambit of his discretion.

The claim was a clinical negligence claim for approximately £3 million. The defendant initially denied liability, but then admitted liability shortly after receiving the court's notice of proposed allocation stating that the case appeared suitable for allocation to the multi-track. The court revoked that form, and ordered judgment to be entered on the admission for an amount to be decided, and scheduled a case management conference (CMC).

The defendant filed and served various documents in advance of the CMC, including a costs budget which (under the then existing rules) had to be filed at least 7 days before the CMC. The claimant's solicitors decided not to file a budget before the CMC despite repeated urging by the defendant's solicitors. At the CMC, the district judge made an order pursuant to CPR 3.14 that the claimant's recoverable costs should be confined to court fees. The claimant applied to the same district judge to vary the order or alternatively for relief from sanctions, but that was dismissed. An appeal to the circuit judge was also dismissed, so the claimant appealed to the Court of Appeal.

The Chronology

Proceedings were issued in 2013. In January 2013 a defence was filed and Northampton County Court sent out the notice of allocation form which stated among other things that the case was suitable for allocation to the multi track.

- The notified the parties that there would be a two-hour long CMC with a time estimate of two hours.
- On the same date the defendant's solicitors filed and served their directions questionnaire, the proposed draft directions and costs budget.
- The claimant did not send the costs budget.
- The defendant's costs lawyers wrote asking the budget (Jackson LJ stated "That was a sensible letter to send). It was no doubt intended to pave the way for discussions about the parties' respective budgets".
- The claimant did not reply in a constructive way. A budget was still not sent.
- The defendant served an updated costs budget and again asked the claimant for their budget.
- The claimant replied stating that a costs draftsman had been instructed to file a budget but they were "just checking with counsel" whether this was a requirement as judgment had been entered.
- The defendant replied stating that their view was that budgets were required. The claimant's solicitors were not persuaded and again they did not serve a budget.

- The case management conference took place. The defendant's budget was approved. The claimant had not filed a budget in advance. However, the claimant's counsel, at that stage produced an unsigned budget and proposed that this budget be used for costs budgeting.
- The defendant's counsel stated that it was not possible to deal with costs budgeting on the basis of a budget that had just been produced.
- The district judge, therefore, made an order confining the costs budget to court fees.
- The claimant made an application for relief from sanctions which was refused by the district judge.
- The claimant appealed to the Circuit Judge and that appeal was disallowed. The judge held that this was obviously a multi track case and a costs budget should have been filed.

The Court of Appeal dismissed the appeal. The first ground of appeal was that a costs budget was not required as the case had ceased to be a multi-track case when the allocation form had been revoked. The court rejected this argument. The revocation had been made because the case was no longer defended on liability, but as a multi-million pound personal injury action it was self-evidently a multi-track case. The parties were therefore required to serve their budgets seven days before the first CMC. The fact that the case had become quantum only litigation did not take the case out of the costs management regime.

This case was clearly a multi track case. The claim was pleaded for some £3 million. The Court of Appeal held that no sensible person could think it could proceed on the fast track. Further the fact that judgment had been obtained did not take the matter outside the costs budgeting regime. The parties were required to file costs budgets. The automatic sanction in rule 3.14 applied.

The second ground of appeal was that the judges below erred in failing to grant relief from sanctions under CPR 3.9. The Court of Appeal stated that the District Judge had erred in finding that "the present case was factually so close to Mitchell that he was bound to refuse relief from sanctions". That was the wrong approach.

However, the parties had agreed that this was wrong when the parties appeared before the Circuit Judge, who had also refused relief from sanctions.

The Court of Appeal held that the Judge had come to an appropriate conclusion. He had applied the threefold test as laid down by the majority in Denton. The Judge had been critical of the claimant's solicitors. He described the actions of the claimant's solicitors as "foolish" and stated:

> "*I have already referred to the four letters which his opponent had written suggesting that the budgets were required. Any sensible solicitor, even if they believed that they were right about the law, would probably have prepared the budget.*"

Jackson LJ considered criticisms of the Judge's findings and rejected them:-

> "*It seems to me that the various harsh comments which the judge made about the solicitor's decision were proper comments for the judge to make. They were plainly relevant to the exercise of the court's discretion under CPR 3.9. They were plainly relevant to the application of the threefold test in Denton.*"

Finally, the Court of Appeal found that there was no good reason for the breach. The claimant argued that the rules had been misinterpreted by the claimant's solicitors but their approach was reasonable.

> "*The judge rejected that argument in strong terms. He was entitled to do so.*"

It was accepted that the district judge's approach was wrong in that he said the present case was so close to Mitchell that he was bound to refuse relief. The claimant submitted that the circuit judge made the same error in re-exercising the court's discretion as to whether to grant relief, in that he treated himself as constrained by Mitchell to refuse relief. The Court of Appeal disagreed. Reading the judgment as a whole, he had properly applied the Denton three-stage test. This was clearly a serious or significant breach, as the failure meant that if relief were granted there would have to be a second costs management hearing at a later date. There was no good reason for the breach; the judge had rejected the submission that the claimant's approach was reasonable though a mis-interpretation of the rules, and he was entitled to do so. The judge had also applied the third stage correctly and reached a decision which was open to him. Although other judges might have been more lenient, there was no error of principle and it was a decision within the ambit of his discretion.

The Court of Appeal noted that any harshness of the order had been mitigated by the fact that the action subsequently settled.

There was clearly a serious breach by the appellant, which would have resulted in there having to be a further CMC, which would be costly and demanding of court time. Management of the case and of costs would have to be done separately, yet they should be dealt with together.

The District Judge and Circuit Judge had rejected in strong terms the appellant's reason for his breach. The court of appeal would not overturn their assessment.

The Circuit Judge had properly set out the guidance in Denton regarding the third part of the test, and had taken account of the factors in CPR 3.9(1)(a) and (b). He had reached a decision open to him. Other judges might have been more lenient, but his decision was within the ambit of his discretion. He had been very critical of the appellant's solicitor's decision not to produce a costs budget. His comments were proper for him to make as part of his exercise of discretion in applying the three-stage test in Denton. The appeal was dismissed.

The key feature of this case is summed up in the first part of Jackson LJ's judgment:

"This is not a case of an overworked solicitor who simply did not get around to the task. It is a case in which the Claimant's solicitor deliberately decided not to file a budget despite repeated urging by the Defendant's solicitors."

A factor in this case was the claimant's failure to provide a budget despite being asked, four times, by the defendant.

It does appear that even after Denton, the Courts still can hold that a party can be limited in their costs if they are late with a costs budget and the Court of Appeal will be reluctant to overturn such a decision.

Intellimedia Systems Ltd v Richards & Ors Ch D (Warren J) 01/02/2017

This case concerned another failure to file costs budget on time, but in this instance the Court granted relief.

A CMC had been listed. The Defendant filed costs budget. The Claimant emailed D to tell them solicitor involved was ill and would file costs budget early. It did after the time limit had expired.

The breach was not trivial. It had risked disrupting the CMC and the conduct of the litigation and caused additional work for the Defendant.

Although one could be sympathetic that the partner fell ill, it could not excuse him from acting professionally. He should have either delegated responsibility or sent the client elsewhere.

If the Claimant had filed the late documents on time, although some of the outstanding issues might have been agreed, they were typically the sort of matters a master would have resolved.

It was appropriate to grant relief. Although the Claimant had been inefficient, the sanction was not proportionate. The Claimant only applied for relief after it was suggested by the Defendant. The Claimant also sought to amend the Particulars of Claim.

It was odd that he had been capable of managing a receivership application but then a few days later could not discharge his duties in the proceedings.

The most important question was whether the late costs budget caused the loss of the CMC. Had the application for amendment not been made the conference could have proceeded on most of the important issues between the parties including timetabling and disclosure. At worst the application would have been stood over. However, the Claimant was ordered to pay the costs of the hearing on an indemnity basis.

Lakhani v Mahmud [2017] EWHC 1713 (Ch)

In this matter a cost budget was filed one day late. This breach was considered serious primarily because of the impact it had on the parties' ability to agree cost budgets, and the fact that a 45-minute Cost Management Conference far exceeded the listed time as the late service of the budget had to be dealt with. The reason provided for the breach was a misinterpretation of the rules regarding the timescale for service of the budget. The court did not consider this an understandable mistake on which to grant Relief.

This case is another example of the courts imposing the so-called "*Mitchell*" sanction for filing a costs budget late, namely that (under CPR 3.14) the party is treated as having filed a budget limited to court fees. It acts as a reminder that where the rules require a budget (or anything else) to be filed a certain number of days before a hearing, this should be "clear" days, meaning that the first and last day of the time period are excluded from the calculation. This means that the deadline may well be a day earlier than it first seems.

The decision also shows that in some cases it may be better for a party to accept there has been a breach and make a prompt application for relief, rather than seeking to argue on weak grounds that there has in fact been compliance.. It also shows that in most cases it will be difficult to appeal successfully against a first instance judge's decision as to whether relief should be granted.

Background

In the present case, the parties were required to file and serve their costs budgets 21 days before the costs and case management conference (CCMC) scheduled for 10 January 2017. The claimants served their budget on 19 December 2016, the correct day. The defendants' budget was filed a day late, on 20 December (being 21 calendar days before the deadline, but not 21 "clear days" as the rules require).

The defendants initially argued in correspondence that the budget was in time, but ultimately accepted that it was not. They did not make an application for relief from sanctions until just before the CCMC. The circuit judge refused the application and the defendants appealed.

The court dismissed the appeal. The judge noted that it was common ground that the appeal was a review not a rehearing and the court should not interfere with a case management decision of this kind unless satisfied the judgment was plainly wrong and fell outside the generous ambit of the trial judge's discretion.

The court rejected the contention that the circuit judge had erred in assessing the seriousness of the breach. He noted that other judges might have taken a different approach, and this was in his view "on the borderline" of sufficient seriousness to warrant refusal of relief, but the court could not properly interfere with the circuit judge's decision on this point.

The judge noted that the evaluation of seriousness or significance of a breach is not a binary question of primary fact, but a "multifactorial question of degree". It is impossible to list the full range of factors that may be relevant, but the judge included within this list:

- The absolute and relative amount of time lost by being late – here although the budget was only one day late, that delay was more significant because the time period for seeking to agree the budgets was already limited by closure of the defendants' solicitors' offices for most of the Christmas and New Year period.

- Whether the delay affected the litigation or was likely to do so. Although in this case the parties had been able to comment on the opponents' budgets despite the delay, the judge was not obliged to treat that as a conclusive factor on the question of seriousness. A court is entitled to consider the risk of difficulty that a failure to meet a deadline has created, even if it has been possible to perform the task required despite the breach.

- The direct consequences of missing the deadline and how it was addressed. The circuit judge was entitled to take into account the distraction caused by the debate over what the time limit was and whether there was a breach, rather than the defendants taking prompt steps to minimise the impact.

The judge also said there was no basis for challenging the circuit judge's conclusion that there was no reasonable excuse for the default. The defendants' solicitors only started to prepare the costs budget after receiving the claimants' costs budget, so on any basis the work was done at the last minute. While some judges might have taken a more charitable view as to the error in calculating time, and whether days had to be "clear days", it could not be said the circuit judge's evaluation was clearly wrong.

The judge also noted, interestingly, that the circuit judge's decision did not operate to deprive the defendants of a trial altogether. He commented that, if that had been the case, the situation would have deserved more detailed scrutiny than the judge gave it. In the circumstances, the judge said it was difficult to criticise the decision as being disproportionate.

Mott & Anor v Long & Anor [2017] EWHC 2130 (TCC)

In this case, as a result of an IT error, the budget was 10 days late. The defendants filed the budget late, after receiving reminders from the claimant. It was not clear why the budget was late but it was partly technical problems, and partly human error.

The judge considered the Denton test and concluded that the breach was serious, saying:

> *"I have come to the following conclusions on the first stage. Firstly, as a pure matter of time, filing a cost budget 10 days late is not of the same relatively modest order of time as being a few hours or even one or two days late. Secondly, the degree of lateness in every case is always to be construed in the context of the particular circumstances of that case. To my mind the circumstances in Lakhani illustrate that point very clearly. Thirdly, I accept Mr Christie's main submission that lateness in serving a cost budget has the capacity to prejudice the very process of co-operation in the cost budgeting process which the rules are designed to achieve. In those circumstances I have come to the conclusion that the period of delay in this case answers the description of being serious or significant, perhaps with particular emphasis on the latter word."*

The Judge clearly thought that 10 days delay was significant and also that the IT system issue was not a good reason. It was only all the circumstances of the case which saved the Defendant. The Judge found that there was no good reason for the breach, saying that:

> *"A reasonable conclusion to draw from the evidence in the defendants' solicitor's witness statement is that the document which she drafted on 6 July was not saved to the defendants' solicitors' IT system. I deliberately use the passive sense in that sentence. It is not clear, on the evidence in the application, whether the failure was hers or someone else's at the defendants' solicitors i.e. a human error, or whether it was a fault in the IT system itself i.e. a system error. There is no detail about what the "IT difficulties" were. In his oral submissions Mr Christie QC submitted that if Plexus were indeed experiencing problems of the magnitude inferred in the defendants' solicitor's witness statement, such problems might have been explained by a witness statement from someone from their IT department or from someone having the relevant or appropriate IT expertise. In my judgement, there is force in that observation.*
>
> *I have therefore come to the conclusion that while there may have been a reason why the failure or default occurred, which might have amounted to a good reason, I am not satisfied on the evidence in the application that the defendants have established that there was good reason for the default."*

As is often the case, the Defendant got home on all the circumstances, the third stage of the Denton test.

> *"To my mind the following are material among the circumstances of the case. Firstly, the fact that the defendants' solicitors have in fact served a cost budget, and have done so some nine days before this CMC....*
>
> *However, I have come to the overall conclusion, having regard to all the circumstances of the case, in particular the reasons set out above as regards the need for the defendant to file and serve a revised cost budget reflecting the substantive orders for directions relating to expert opinion evidence and the estimated length of the forthcoming trial which the court has now made, that this is a case where I should grant the defendants relief from sanction. The fact that the parties are now in precisely the same procedural position in which they would*

> *have been so far as the process of cost budgeting is concerned, had the defendants served their cost budget in time, is a highly significant circumstance in the case, and one to which the court should have proper regard.*
>
> *However, such relief from sanction will come at a cost to the defendants. I will order that they are to pay the claimants' costs of and occasioned by the application, and I will now hear from counsel precisely what such an order to costs may or may not involve."*

This resulted in the parties having insufficient time to prepare a meaningful budget discussion report. Importantly, the court was in agreement with the Defendant that regardless of the breach, the budgets could not have been agreed at the Cost Management Conference. This was because as a result of converging directions, revised budgets would have been sought in any event.

Therefore, relief was granted but the Defendant was ordered to pay the costs of the application. A significant factor was the fact that a second costs budget hearing would probably have been needed in any event, regardless of the defendant's default.

Freeborn v Marcal [2017] EWHC 3046 (TCC)

In this case, the High Court penalised a claimant in costs for requiring the defendant to apply for relief from sanctions, where the defendant had relied on a letter from the court which arguably set out the wrong date for filing costs budgets.

The court emphasised that, following the court's tougher approach to granting relief from sanctions established in Mitchell and Denton (as outlined here), it is extremely important for parties to ensure that they comply with the CPR. However, parties should not abuse this tougher approach. Parties need to consider whether it is proportionate and appropriate to require their opponent to make an application for relief from sanctions, or to oppose that application, in all the circumstances of the case.

This judgment is consistent with the warning in Denton that the courts are willing to penalise parties who try to hold their opponents to what the court sees as an overly strict approach to compliance with rules and court orders, in order to gain a tactical advantage, and highlights the need for litigants to strike a fine balance when responding to applications for relief or requests to extend time.

Background

The court wrote to the parties identifying the date for the case management conference (CMC) and stating that the parties were required to file and exchange costs budgets not less than seven days before the CMC. This was, however, the time limit under the old version of CPR 3.13; the current version provides that "unless the court otherwise orders, all parties...must file and exchange budgets...not later than 21 days before the first case management conference".

The claimant served its costs budget 21 days before the CMC, in accordance with the current version of CPR 3.13. However, the defendant relied on the letter from the court office and therefore served its costs budget just seven days before the CMC. The claimant then suggested not having raised the point earlier that the defendant's budget should have been provided 14 days earlier and therefore the court should apply the sanction for late filing of budgets set out in CPR 3.14, restricting recoverable costs.

Due to the claimant's approach, the defendant was forced to make a formal application for relief from sanctions, in case it was not entitled to rely on the letter from the court.

Decision

The court held that, in the circumstances, the defendant was not required to make an application for relief from sanctions. CPR 3.13

states that costs budgets must be filed and exchanged not later than 21 days before the first CMC “unless the court orders otherwise”. Here, the court’s letter amounted to the court ordering otherwise.

As the defendant filed its cost budget within the date set out in that letter, the defendant had complied with CPR 3.13. It was immaterial that the court’s letter may have erroneously contained the deadline set out in the old version of CPR 3.13 (seven rather than 21 days before the CMC). The judge commented: “A busy litigation solicitor is entitled simply to rely on the date specified in writing by the court office, rather than embarking on an investigation into whether or not the letter contained an error.”

In any event, if relief from sanctions was needed, the claimant would have satisfied the three-stage test set out in Denton: (i) the breach was not serious and significant; (ii) there was good reason for the delay (given that it stemmed from the court’s error); and (iii) in all the circumstances, it was just and reasonable to grant relief.

The claimant was criticised for requiring the defendant to make an application for relief from sanctions and was ordered to pay the defendant’s costs of the application. The judge noted:

“It is, of course, extremely important, post-Mitchell and post-Denton, for the parties to civil litigation to ensure that they comply with the CPR. Courts will be far less forgiving of non-compliance than they ever used to be. But that tougher approach must not be abused in the way that occurred here. Parties need to consider carefully whether the alleged breach of the rules is, on analysis, any such thing and, even if it is, whether it is proportionate and appropriate to require or oppose an application for relief from sanctions in all the circumstances of the case.”

Conclusion

Since the Jackson reforms, the court's approach to procedural failings has softened from the somewhat draconian approach taken in the aftermath of the high-profile Mitchell decision in November 2013, in particular in light of the Court of Appeal's "clarification" of the Mitchell guidance in its Denton decision in July 2014. There are fewer cases in which parties attempt to take their opponents to task for minor breaches now, partly because costs sanctions may be imposed on those who seek to take unreasonable advantage of an opponent's breach.

However, it is by no means a cakewalk for those who fail to comply with court rules and orders. The cases on late filing of costs budgets highlight the continued scope for hard decisions, and the Court of Appeal's reluctance to interfere with a lower court's decision in this field.

The cases also act as a reminder that costs budgets must be filed in time or a party risks facing serious restrictions on its recoverable costs. If in doubt as to whether a budget is required, the safest bet is to assume that it is.

Before his retirement, Jackson was promulgating fixed recoverable costs for cases. No doubt there will be sanctions applicable for breach of these new rules and further litigation will ensue.

Summary points to note

- Start work on budgets as soon as you can.
- Discuss budgets and assumptions with the other side.
- If you miss the deadline for filing your budget, your client's recoverable costs will be limited to court fees unless you obtain relief from sanction.
- If in doubt as to whether a budget is required, serve one.
- Use key date systems to record and monitor deadlines and timetables. Ensure all staff know that this is essential.

- Ensure external providers such as costs draftsmen know the deadlines they must meet and the consequences of failure.

- If you know you are going to struggle to meet a deadline apply for an extension of time before the date has passed, not relief from sanctions afterwards.

- If you are at the receiving end of an application don't be seen to be taking advantage of the other party's late service of a Costs budget.

CHAPTER FOUR
LITIGANTS IN PERSON

The rising number of Litigants in Person following legal aid cuts, the increase in the small-claims limit, and the introduction of employment tribunal fees is well-documented. Civil Justice Statistics published on 2 June 2016 record that, in 2015, both the claimant and defendant had legal representation in only 58% of defended cases.

The proportion of applications to the Court of Appeal for permission to appeal by litigants in person (LIPs) has gone up by 50% in the last 10 years, the Master of the Rolls has said.

It is also notable that relief from sanctions also applies in tribunals where many cases are dealt with in person as litigants cannot afford representation.

In a speech on civil justice reform after the retirement of Sir Rupert Jackson, Sir Terence Etherton also said that costs reform would not stop with Sir Rupert's retirement, and that the demands on civil justice were increasing, driven by continued growth in the numbers of litigants in person, growth of the digital economy, the cost of litigation and unmet need.

> *"First, and most obviously, we see the continued growth in litigants in person as a result of changes to legal aid provision and the cost of litigation."*

Sir Terence said a "significant amount" had been said about litigants in person, and the issue was

> *"one which, perhaps surprisingly to many, is of concern even in my own court, the civil division of the Court of Appeal, where the number of permission to appeal applications brought by litigants in person stood at 42% in the 12 months ended 31 January 2018."*

> *"The comparable figure in 2007/2008 was just under 28%. Reform is needed to ensure that we can deliver justice effectively for this increasing group of litigants."*

Litigants in person are appearing more frequently in the civil courts and tribunals including the Court of Appeal. These developments have an impact on the operation of courts and on the lawyers representing the other side in a case. The idea of the proposed Online Court and the existing Small Claims Track is to make the Courts available to people without having to instruct lawyers. When the Civil Liability Bill becomes law it is possible that low value personal injury claims may be pursued by litigants without representation. A man who is his own lawyer has a fool for a client is the old adage. Certainly litigants in person are more likely to misunderstand the law and to miss deadlines.

The disadvantages suffered by litigants in person are set out in the Equal Treatment Benchbook, published in 2018.

In 2013, a judicial working party chaired by Mr Justice Hickinbottom summed up the position as follows:

> *"Providing access to justice for litigants in person within the constraints of a system that has been developed on the basis that most litigants will be legally represented poses considerable and unique challenges for the judiciary. Cases will inevitably take more time, during a period of severe pressure on judicial time. However, litigants in person are not in themselves 'a problem'; the problem lies with a system which has not developed with a focus on unrepresented litigants. We consider it vital that, despite the enormous challenge presented, judges are enabled and empowered to adapt the system to the needs of litigants in person, rather than vice versa"*

How then are litigants in person treated in relation to compliance with Court order and directions? Are they and should they be treated differently than represented parties, with one set of rules for one and one for another?

In my submission, people who don't have lawyers should not be expected to deal with litigation in exactly the same way, as if this was a full-time job. I have met litigants, as a mediator, who have other work to do and simply don't have time to deal with Court orders, working on their cases at the evening or weekends. Giving them a bit more leeway is just a way of levelling the playing field.

One way the Courts can assist without bending the rules is to make sure that litigants in person understand what they need to do and by when, in the first place. Hence it is often necessary to explain how a witness statement should be drafted and signed with a statement of truth. The Equal Treatment Benchbook explains:

> "*The aim is to ensure that litigants in person understand what is going on and what is expected of them at all stages of the proceedings – before, during and after any attendances at a hearing. This means ensuring that:*
>
> • *The process is (or has been) explained to them in a manner that they can understand.*
>
> • *They have access to appropriate information (e.g. the rules, practice directions and guidelines – whether from publications or websites).*
>
> • *They are informed about what is expected of them in ample time for them to prepare and comply.*
>
> • *Wherever possible, they are given sufficient time for their particular needs*
>
> *Where pre-hearing directions are given in writing, litigants in person may not understand exactly what they are supposed to do, or they may not have the skill-set to do it correctly.*
>
> *In conducting case management hearings, it is useful to:*

• *Start by explaining this is only a case management hearing, not a hearing to decide what happened in their case.*

• *Explain every direction or court order clearly, not only by avoiding jargon, but by anticipating common misunderstandings.*

• *Involve litigants in person in the process of giving directions (eg asking them how much time they need to take a particular step and why) so that they realise how the directions relate to the conduct of their own case.*

• *Check that the LIP understands, by asking the LIP to feed back what he or she must now do and on what date.*

• *Do not simply ask 'Do you understand?' LIPs might say 'yes' out of embarrassment or because they wrongly believe they do understand, or to save face. Saving face is a universal concept, but this can be a particularly important issue for certain cultures....*

• *Make realistic directions given the capabilities of the LIP in question. Offer hands-on help if appropriate, eg in identifying the exact nature of the claim. Where possible, engage the help of the represented party, eg in making the first draft of a list of issues, or putting together a proposed trial bundle.*

• *At the end of the case management hearing, go back over key dates and actions and check the LIP has written them down.*

• *Confirm the directions/orders in writing as soon as possible after the case management hearing, so that the LIP receives the letter in good time to prepare for the earliest required action, and to take advice if needed. This might involve asking for the case management letter to go out as a priority.*

• *As well as orders, include in the case management letter, key points of explanation or advice on procedure which the LIP might otherwise forget.*

> • *Make any reasonable adjustments required if the LIP is disabled. It is not only at the final hearing / trial that such adjustments may need to be made. Disabled LIPs may be less assertive about raising their needs than where there they have representation.*
>
> • *Similarly, if English is not the LIP's first language, check whether an interpreter is necessary.... These considerations do not only apply to the final hearing / trial."*

Nonetheless, it is not always possible for the Judge to go into this level of detail or to give the Litigant in Person such a high degree of attention in the amount of time permitted. Despite best endeavours Litigants in Person still fail to comply with directions, for example getting confused about "filing" and "service" and certainly not understanding about "clear days" before a hearing. Fortunately they do not have to comply with costs management rules although I have seen costs budgets produced by LIPs setting out their costs at the LIP rate.

What then if you/they are in breach as a LIP and how to deal with an application for relief from sanction? The Equal Treatment Benchbook makes the following recommendations:

> "*Compliance with directions/orders*
>
> *Given the greater emphasis in the current Civil Procedure Rules on enforcement of rules and orders, it is crucial that litigants in person understand both what is required of them and the consequences of non-compliance.*
>
> *LIPs do not necessarily realise that court orders are more than aspirational. They may also fail to understand that if they do not comply with an order, they are at risk of being struck out. Although standard letters advise of the consequences of non-compliance, a LIP may not have read the letter to the end, or retained what it said, or understood the formal words and jargon involved ('non-compliance', 'strike out' etc). In addition, they may have become embroiled in heated cor-*

respondence with the other side, and have lost track of the overall picture.

LIPs may also not understand the automatic effect of an 'Unless Order'.

There is also the possibility that the LIP does understand the risk, but simply does not know how to comply with the order. 'Unless Orders', in particular, should be made with great care where there is a possibility that the LIP does not understand how to comply, as opposed to being unwilling to do so.

Having said that, cases do need to be prepared and the other side is entitled to a level of information and cooperation. It is a question of enabling LIPs to do what is necessary, without excessively indulging any failure to cooperate.

LIPs can become very agitated if the other side does not comply on time with pre-hearing directions. Sometimes LIPs believe that, if the other side has failed to comply on time with such directions, that in itself is evidence in support of their own case, or that the opponent should be prevented from defending or proceeding further. They often feel upset at what they regard as an over- tolerant attitude by the court or tribunal to delays by solicitors. The reasons for any decision to extend time for the represented party should therefore be carefully explained."

One question which arises is whether a litigant in person should be treated any differently to other litigants in respect of breaches of orders or directions. The Civil Procedure Rules provide that regard should be given in case management to the fact that a party is represented:

3.1A

(1) This rule applies in any proceedings where at least one party is unrepresented.

(2) When the court is exercising any powers of case management, it must have regard to the fact that at least one party is unrepresented.

The professional bodies also suggest that a more understanding approach should be adopted when dealing with LIPs. In June 2015, the Law Society in conjunction with the Bar Council and CILEX produced a guide to litigants in person. It provides some guidance, as follows:

"A LiP might ask for an adjournment or an extension of time in circumstances where a lawyer may believe that no adjournment or extension is necessary or that the circumstances behind the application are primarily or wholly of the LiP's making. For example, a LiP genuinely might not appreciate the importance of the attendance of witnesses. In terms of helping the court process go more smoothly, it may be useful to try to anticipate such requests, for instance, by explaining to the LiP, or inviting the court to explain to the LiP, in advance, their responsibility to secure the attendance of witnesses.

The granting of an adjournment or extension is always a matter of discretion and courts may more readily grant an application when it is sought by a LiP. It is appropriate to be ready to consent to a reasonable request (whether from a LiP or a represented party) where the rules allow. Bear in mind that appellate courts are particularly concerned to ensure that LiPs are given every opportunity to present their case, in so far as that is consistent with fairness.

A judge is likely to grant an adjournment or extension where a submission or issue catches a LiP by surprise, so providing the LiP with reasonable advance notice could forestall such an application.

Failure to comply with case management/procedural orders

When an order is made, it is helpful if the court can be clear about the consequences of non-compliance, including that costs may be sought against the LiP and the quantum of those costs. If you can see that a LiP is heading towards non-compliance, you should consider drawing this to the LiP's attention. The court might give a LiP less

> *leeway if it is aware that the LiP has been reminded of the court's requirements and the possible consequences of non-compliance."*

So, the general gist of the advice is to explain things clearly to litigants in person and be reasonable in order to get the Court on side.

In practice, the cases show that when grappling with the dilemma of non-compliance by litigants in person the Courts are in fact unwilling to lean over backwards too much and to operate a dual track system.

Whilst the rules now place increased emphasis on the need for compliance with court rules, orders and directions, there is a concern to provide access to justice and the challenges that can arise with increasing numbers of litigants in person.

Jones v Longley

In Jones v Longley, it was held that the Courts "cannot and do not" modify the rules for those who are unrepresented.

Jones v Longley was a Part 8 claim by the executor of a will for an order, under the Administration of Justice Act 1985, to remove the first defendant (D1) as co-executor. Subsequently, D1 (a litigant in person) was given permission to file and serve a counterclaim.

Initially, D1 filed a "counterclaim" (17 pages) plus another 80-page document which referred to other documents totalling about 2,000 pages. The documents were in a "pedantic and prolix, meandering" style and lacked particularity in important places. Further, there were no headings or paragraph numbers although the paragraphs were often very long. The documents did not comply with the relevant procedural rules, practice directions and other guidance.

D1 was given a "second bite of the cherry". At a hearing on 30 July 2015, Master Matthews directed D1 to file and serve on the claimant:

> *"a brief statement of case summarising his counterclaim, which shall comply with the requirements of part 16 of the Civil Procedure Rules 1998 and its Practice Direction, and with the requirements of Chapter 2 and Appendix 2 of the Chancery Guide".*

On 9 November, the claimant applied to strike out the revised counterclaim, under CPR 3.4(2)(a) and (b), on the basis that it did not comply with the procedural rules or the master's order.

On the hearing of the application, Master Matthews saw "force" in the three key criticisms:

- The counterclaim was too dense and prolix to allow a point by point response.
- It mixed together claims in different capacities against different parties.
- The claims were not properly particularised, and there was no coherent case on causation. Further, the counterclaim was still formally defective.

Taking account of the Denton principles, and looking "in the round", Master Matthews asked himself why he should grant a further indulgence to a party who showed no signs of understanding what was wrong with the statement of case, or of obtaining advice, who had not applied for the necessary permission to bring a counterclaim against third parties, and whose case seemed "at best weak".

The Judge noted the need to consider the position of the claimant who had had allegations hanging over him for some years and of other litigants waiting for their cases to be dealt with.

He also observed that courts' resources are "sadly limited" and there must come a point when litigants in one case have had as much of the resources as is proportionate. He recognised that it is "a strong thing" to strike out a statement of case, particularly that of a litigant in person, but concluded that he should strike out the counterclaim as an abuse of the court's process or otherwise likely to obstruct the just disposal of the proceedings (under CPR 3.4(2)(b).

Interestingly, at paragraphs 56 to 59 of his judgment, Master Matthews specifically addressed "The position of litigants in person".

He identified this as a case where "many, perhaps most" of the problems arose from the fact that the Defendant was not a qualified lawyer and appeared to have no experience of this type of litigation.

On the other hand, surely the Courts, as a public service, should be open to all whether they are represented or not? For example it is never argued that to see a doctor you should be accompanied by a patient advocate.

In this case, the master was in no doubt about the appropriate approach:

He saw it as "desirable to stress" that there are not separate procedural rules for those who are legally represented and those who are not, and that the courts "cannot and do not" modify the rules for those who are unrepresented. Although there might be a little more leeway for litigants in person "at the margins", where judges are exercising their discretion (or in cases where the application of a rule might be affected by lack of knowledge or experience of the legal process), such cases are "rare".

The Master saw it as significant that the counterclaim in issue was a revised version produced after comments by the court and criticisms by the claimant. In his view, the Defendant knew what was wrong with the first draft and had had a second chance, by taking advice, or considering the relevant rules, to produce a compliant counterclaim.

The Master was critical of the drafting of the counterclaim. However, interestingly, he saw the need to include in his judgment an explanation of what the wording of his own order giving the Defendant a "second bite of the cherry" had been intended to achieve.

He explained that his "intention" had been that the Defendant should prepare "a short but well-organised statement of his counterclaim, which could refer to and use the existing counterclaim as voluntary further particulars, thus acting not only as a statement of case in its own right, but also as a kind of road-map and index to the existing documents, which need not then be wasted." He noted that the Defendant "appear[ed] however to have misunderstood my purpose", and had understood that the original counterclaim would stand as the particulars of the claim, with a short summary "to aid transparency".

The Master's order did make clear the need for compliance with the relevant procedural requirements, referring to CPR 16, PD 16 and additional guidance in the Chancery Guide. This shows the complexity of our current court rules. How is a litigant in person, recognised as apparently having no experience of this type of litigation, be expected to look at three separate places in order to get the full picture regarding the procedural requirements? This raises the question of who the procedural rules should be aimed at: judges, lawyers, or the parties themselves, particularly given the significant increase in litigants in person.

There is some concern that the new online Court will be a "lawyer less" process designed for litigants in person. Certainly the new online Money Claims system seems easy to use. Many will consider this to be a good thing, reducing cost and complexity.

The master recognised the seriousness of striking out a statement of case, particularly of a litigant in person, but concluded that it was appropriate in all the circumstances of this case. It may be that the fact that the Defendant's counterclaim appeared "at best weak" made the master more relaxed about striking out the counterclaim. Nonetheless, this was robust case management.

Barons Bridging Finance

In this case, it was relevant that the party was a litigant in person. Here, the appellants, including Mr Gopee (the third appellant, a litigant in person) challenged a declaration that an assignment of the book debts of the respondent, Barons Finance Ltd, was void under section 127 of the Insolvency Act, having been made after the commencement of the company's winding up or, even if that were not the case, should be set aside (a) under section 238 of the Act as a transaction at an undervalue and (b) under section 423 as a transaction to defraud creditors.

The issue on appeal was whether Mr Gopee had had a fair trial on the issue of the validity of the assignment. The key complaints were that the judge below had refused to entertain Mr Gopee's disclosure application, issued seven days before the trial, and had also refused to allow Mr Gopee to rely on a four-page witness statement and 104-page exhibit, that he produced at the hearing. No good reason had been given for the delay or the failure to seek an extension.

What is striking is the different tone adopted by the Court of Appeal, when considering the position of Mr Gopee as a litigant in person. Notwithstanding he was recognised as having had "to put it mildly, somewhat of a chequered career in the courts in relation to his conduct of the company and his other associated money lending companies", the court here seemed to be willing to temper the rules due to his lack of legal representation.

At paragraph 40 of the judgment, Lady Justice Gloster observed that, where Mr Gopee (who "albeit an experienced litigant, was acting as a litigant in person") had filed a defence and witness statement denying the backdating and the transfer at an undervalue, it was wrong for the judge not to have allowed him to give evidence. She held that the judge should have allowed Mr Gopee to go into the witness box and give evidence in chief in order to support his defence and be subjected to cross-examination, or the judge should have accepted his additional witness statements as evidence and allowed him to be cross-examined on them.

The approach of the Court of Appeal, seems to have been much more Litigant in Person friendly. In our view there is a need for a more consistent approach by the courts, and there is a challenge of making civil procedural rules simpler and more easily navigable by court users.

Barton v Wright Hassall LLP

The lack of consistency is illustrated by the Supreme Court decision in Barron v Wright Hassall LLP in which there was little leniency shown for a litigant in person who failed to follow the rules on service of a claim form.

In this case Mr Barton, a litigant in person, attempted to serve a claim form on the defendant's solicitors by email but he did not obtain prior confirmation that they would accept service in this way.

Accordingly, service was not compliant with the Civil Procedure Rules.

Mr Barton was in dispute with the firm Wright Hassall LLP (the defendant) and solicitors for the firm emailed him asking him to send all correspondence to them and saying they would "await service of the claim form and particulars of claim".

The claim form could have been served on the defendant by the court but Mr Barton chose to serve it himself. Under CPR 7.5 he had four months in which to do so, after the date of issue of the claim form. This was the period during which the claim form was valid. If he did not serve within this timeframe, his ability to bring the claim would be lost because it would be time-barred under the law on limitation.

On the day before expiry of the claim form Mr Barton emailed the solicitors for the defendant attaching the documents "by means of service". He received an automatic reply with a number to contact in case of urgency, which he did not use.

The defendant's solicitors replied 10 days later to say they had not confirmed they would accept service by email and it was not a permitted mode of service. The claim form had, therefore, expired without proper service and the claim was statute barred.

Under CPR Part 6, where a document is to be served by email, the party who is to be served or their solicitor must previously have indicated in writing that they are willing to accept service by email. An email address set out on their writing paper will be taken as an indication of willingness to accept email service but only where it is stated that the email address may be used for service. This is, in my view, an archaic rule which litigants in person will struggle with in the Internet Age. Any ordinary person would think that emailing a document to someone counts as Service of that document.

Mr Barton's case was that his service by email was valid: the email he received from the defendant's solicitors saying they awaited service indicated they were willing to be served by email. Alternatively, he asked for service to be validated by the court under CPR 6.15(2); this required there to be a good reason for authorising bad service. In the further alternative he asked for validity of the claim form to be extended so he would have more time to serve it properly.

In the County Court, Mr Barton failed on all three grounds. The judge held that the only reason why Mr Barton did not comply with the rules on service was that he did not know what those rules were, and that was not a good reason to make the requested order. Mr Barton was given permission to appeal but only on the ground that service be validated by the court under CPR 6.15(2).

Mr Barton's appeals failed in both the High Court and the Court of Appeal and his final appeal was to the Supreme Court.

The Supreme Court said that what constituted a "good reason" for validating service was essentially a matter of factual evaluation.

Generally speaking, the main factors in deciding there was a 'good reason' were whether the claimant had taken reasonable steps to effect service in accordance with the rules, whether the defendant or its solicitor was aware of the contents of the claim form at the time when it expired and whether the defendant would suffer any prejudice by the retrospective validation of a non-compliant service of the claim form, bearing in mind what it knew about its contents.

The court held:

It was not enough that Mr Barton's email successfully brought the claim form to the attention of the defendant's solicitors because the manner of service was important. Service within the period of validity of the claim form has implications for limitation periods. Time stops running for limitation purposes when a claim form is issued;

A lack of legal representation will often justify making allowances in making case management decisions and in conducting hearings. However, it will not usually justify allowing litigants a lower standard of compliance with rules or orders of the court. The rules provide a framework within which the interests of both sides must be balanced. Unless the rules and practice directions are particularly inaccessible or obscure (and the court found the relevant rules in this case were not), it is reasonable to expect a litigant in person to familiarise himself with the rules which apply to any step which he is about to take. The Court found that:

> "*The overriding objective requires the courts so far as practicable to enforce compliance with the rules: CPR rule 1.1(1)(f). The rules do not in any relevant respect distinguish between represented and unrepresented parties.*"

The judge observed that any advantage enjoyed by a litigant in person imposed a corresponding disadvantage on the other side, "which may be significant if it affects the latter's legal rights, under the Limitation Acts for example".

By the time it came to serve his claim, Mr Barton was an experienced litigant. He knew about limitation periods and that not all solicitors accepted service by email. However, he took no steps to check whether the defendant's solicitors did so, or to see what the rules regarding service by email were.

Although it was not a point being appealed, the court said that it did not consider the email from the defendant's solicitors saying they awaited service was an indication of willingness to accept service by email. Also, it rejected the suggestion that the firm was 'playing technical games' with Mr Barton by taking the point.

Mr Barton did not issue the claim form until the very end of the limitation period and he opted not to have it served by the court. In the view of the Supreme Court, "A person who courts disaster in this way can have only a very limited claim on the court's indulgence in an application under CPR rule 6.15(2)". In conclusion, it found that there was no good reason why Mr Barton should be absolved from his errors at the defendant's expense.

This decision has to be correct to avoid the floodgates being opened for litigants in person who have failed to understand or observe the rules and their implications.

However, Lord Briggs, who gave a dissenting judgment, expressed concern that the meaning and effect of CPR 6.15 had come before the Supreme Court twice in recent years and that this time its meaning had divided the court. We would echo his concerns: there are many parts of the CPR that are less intelligible than rule 6.15 and with more rules and detail being added each year, it is becoming an increasingly difficult task for legal practitioners to keep account of the changes. It must be considerably more difficult for litigants in person to know what is required.

The barrister who acted for Mr Barton, said: "The narrow majority by which our client's case was lost reflects the difficulty judges have in deciding when to apply the dispensing provision for invalid service and what 'special' treatment, if any, should be afforded to litigants in person.

> "*We are actively considering an application to the European Court of Human Rights on article 6 grounds, namely that an "excessive formalism" has caused the loss if Mr Barton's claim.*"

A spokesman for the Access to Justice campaign group, said the decision had implications for the government's plan to raise the small claims limit for personal injury cases.

> "*The Supreme Court [has confirmed] that ignorance of the law is no defence, making it more likely that, if the personal injury reforms become law, LiPs will have their cases struck out because they will not be able to access expert legal advice as is the case at the moment.*"
>
> "*The government's determination to press ahead with the Civil Liability Bill will make a bad situation much worse...*"
>
> "*Now, the government will be required to make the current arcane process LiP-friendly, a herculean task given the number of different elements within a personal injury claim any new system will need to incorporate.*"

EDF Energy Customers Ltd v Re-Energized Ltd [2018] EWHC 652 (Ch)

In this case, HHJ Paul Matthews (sitting as a High Court Judge) carried out a comprehensive review of the authorities relating to the latitude to be afforded to litigants in person. It shows clearly that the fact that a litigant was unrepresented does not give it any special status, nor is at liberty to argue, on appeal, that the case could have been argued differently below.

> "*I bear in mind also that a litigant in person is not the only party to consider. I must also consider the position of the represented party and*

> *the public generally. Every indulgence given to a litigant in person casts an extra burden on the represented party and on the court system. This extra burden is usually marginal, but it mounts up over time. Yet a represented party too may have limited resources, and may have had to make choices, indeed sometimes sacrifices too, in allocating resources so as to be able to afford representation. Delays and lack of finality may impose unwanted and unwarrantable costs on him or her too. The same is true of the court system."*

A company, acting without legal representations, appealed against a winding up order. The respondent creditor had sent out a statutory demand. The company made an application to restrain advertisement of the petition. That application was refused. In correspondence with the creditor's solicitors it was pointed out to the company directors that the application to restrain an advertisement was a different application to that opposing the petition, although the principles to be considered, were largely the same.

The company then attended at the hearing for winding up. The District Judge held that most of the points taken by the company had been decided against it in the failed application to restrain advertisement. A winding up order was made.

The grounds of appeal as filed were that:

> "*The hearing on 18 July was procedurally and substantively unfair such that the debtor was not given a fair hearing or any proper opportunity to advance its opposition to the petition*"

The judge carried out a detailed review of the cases relating to the treatment of litigants in person and concluded.

> "*From these authorities I derive the following principles:*
>
> *1. There is a general duty on tribunals to assist litigants, depending on the circumstances, but it is for the tribunal to decide what this*

duty requires in any particular case and how best to fulfil it, whilst remaining impartial.

2. The fact that a litigant is acting in person is not in itself a reason to disapply procedural rules or orders or directions, or excuse non-compliance with them.

3. The granting of a special indulgence to a litigant in person may be justified where a rule is hard to find or it is difficult to understand, or it is ambiguous.

4. There may be some leeway given to a litigant in person at the margins when the court is considering relief from sanctions or promptness in applying to set aside an order."

So the Judge concluded that there should be no "special treatment" for litigants in person as the rules in the part of the law his case concerned were neither hard to find nor "particularly difficult to understand." The judge said the interests of the represented party and the public also had to be taken into account.

He described Mr Watson as an "articulate and knowledgeable layman", but bore in mind that he chose not to seek legal advice, including on some letters from the respondent's solicitors which he misconstrued.

HHJ Matthews said: "What the solicitor said [in the letters] was correct as far as it went. He could have said more (indeed, he could have said rather less), but there was no duty, as Mr Watson accepts, on those solicitors to advise him as the adverse party. In my judgment those emails were not misleading, and do not alter the basic position."

He said the rules in this part of the law were not hard to find or "particularly difficult" to understand.

"Of course, I accept that a layman without any experience of finding his way round a law book or the statute book will take longer to do so, and may fall into error more easily and more frequently than a

> *trained lawyer. That is, after all, why it takes training to become a lawyer."*
>
> *"Yet Mr Watson had been able to put together a sensible skeleton argument and a bundle for the injunction hearing, a written argument before the district judge, and also a bundle for this appeal. That was of course his choice, as to how he allocated the company's available resources."*
>
> *"But he cannot complain if it does not produce the result he wished for."*

The judge said he had also to consider the position of the represented party and the public generally.

> *"Every indulgence given to a litigant in person casts an extra burden on the represented party and on the court system. This extra burden is usually marginal, but it mounts up over time.*
>
> *"Yet a represented party too may have limited resources, and may have had to make choices, indeed sometimes sacrifices too, in allocating resources so as to be able to afford representation. Delays and lack of finality may impose unwanted and unwarrantable costs on him or her too. The same is true of the court system..."*
>
> *"So, overall, in my view there should be no special treatment for Mr Watson here because he was a litigant in person at first instance."*

Clarke v Revenue and Customs [2018] UKFTT 123 (TC)

The Denton principles were also considered by the First-Tier Tribunal Tax Chamber in This case and we look at two relevant particular parts of the judgment: (i) the relevance of reliance on an advisor; whether a litigant in person should be treated differently.

> *"The risk of a poorly performing representative must (in general) fall on the litigant appointing that representative and not on the other party to the appeal."*

The applicant lodged appeals against assessments relating to underpayment of income tax. He acted using an adviser. No correspondence was sent to the applicant directly. That adviser failed to comply with certain orders and the appeals were struck out. An application for reinstatement was not successful. The appellant instructed new advisers who, a year after the last hearing, applied for permission out of time to refuse to reinstate the income tax appeals.

The relevance of reliance on an advisor

The judge considered arguments based around the Denton principles in detail. She also considered an argument that the appellant was acting by his adviser and should not be held responsible for those defaults.

Ms Frawley's case was that Mr Clarke should not be held accountable for the failings of his representative. Her case was that Mr Clarke was not aware of the deadlines and should not be punished because they were missed.

The Court did not agree.

> *"While an appellant does nothing wrong in seeking to appoint a representative, the appellant has chosen to bring legal proceedings, and must accept the responsibility to pursue them as directed by the Tribunal. The appointment of a representative does not absolve the appellant from such a duty: that would be unfair on the other litigant, who has no choice over whether the appellant appoints a representative or as to who that representative is. It is the litigant who appoints a representative who must (in general at least) take the burden as well as the benefit of what his representative does (or fails to do) in his appeal. The risk of a poorly performing representative must (in general) fall on the litigant appointing that representative and not on the other party to the appeal. To rule otherwise is mani-*

festly unfair to HMRC, who had no choice or control of Mr Clarke's decision to appoint a representative, and to whom the appellant's representative owes no duty of care.

Ms Frawley suggested the position is different where the appointed representative was not legally qualified and not insured. She pointed out that the CPR would not allow someone who was not a legal representative and professionally qualified (or equivalent) to represent a person in court: she suggested the Tribunal or HMRC should bear responsibility for Mr Clarke's choice of Mr Horler because the Tribunal rules permit anyone (whether legally qualified or subject to a professional body and whether or not insured) to represent a taxpayer in the Tribunal.

I do not agree that that is a reason for shifting liability for the appellant's representative's defaults to the respondents. It is the appellant's choice who to appoint as representative. He must take responsibility for his choice. It is not for the respondent to underwrite the appellant's choice of an unqualified and uninsured representative. And while the Tribunal's rules, no doubt intended to improve access to justice, permit the appointment of an unqualified and uninsured representative, it is not responsible where the appellant chooses such a representative.

While I accept that Mr Clarke chose someone recommended to him, and that for the first 12 months or so after the appointment he had no cause to complain about his representative, nevertheless he knew or ought to have known that Mr Horler held no professional qualification, was not professionally supervised, and was not insured. It was his choice to appoint him."

Should litigants in person be treated more leniently?

Ms Frawley also suggested that Mr Clarke should be treated as a litigant in person (as he was not legally represented) and that the courts were and should be more lenient to a litigant in person. In reality, this amounted to much the same as the previous proposition that Mr

Clarke should not be held accountable for the failures of his unqualified and uninsured representative.

The day before the hearing, although none of us were aware of it at the time, the Supreme Court issued its decision in Barton v Wright Hassall LLP [2018] UKSC 12 where the court said:

[18]…[Litigants in person's] lack of representation will often justify making allowances in making case management decisions and in conducting hearings. But it will not usually justify applying to litigants in person a lower standard of compliance with rules or orders of the court. The overriding objective requires the courts so far as practicable to enforce compliance with the rules: CPR rule 1.1(1)(f). The rules do not in any relevant respect distinguish between represented and unrepresented parties. In applications under CPR 3.9 for relief from sanctions, it is now well established that the fact that the applicant was unrepresented at the relevant time is not in itself a reason not to enforce rules of court against him: R (Hysaj) v Secretary of State for the Home Department [2015] 1 WLR 2472, para 44 (Moore-Bick LJ); Nata Lee Ltd v Abid [2015] 2 P & CR 3,[2014] EWCA Civ 1652. At best, it may affect the issue "at the margin", as Briggs LJ observed (para 53) in the latter case, which I take to mean that it may increase the weight to be given to some other, more directly relevant factor. It is fair to say that in applications for relief from sanctions, this is mainly because of what I have called the disciplinary factor, …. The rules provide a framework within which to balance the interest of both sides. That balance is inevitably disturbed if an unrepresented litigant is entitled to greater indulgence in complying with them than his represented opponent. Any advantage enjoyed by a litigant in person imposes a corresponding disadvantage on the other side, which may be significant if it affects the latter's legal rights, under the Limitation Acts for example. Unless the rules and practice directions are particularly inaccessible or obscure, it is reasonable to expect a litigant in person to familiarise himself with the rules which apply to any step which he is about to take.

The gist of this is that, while the Tribunal will do what it can to assist litigants in person, by and large litigants in person have no extra leniency in respect of compliance with the rules and directions of the Tribunal, although their status as litigants in person might have relevance in marginal cases where it is an explanation for the default.

But I do not see that as being of assistance to Mr Clarke. He was not a litigant in person: his defaults were not because he was inexperienced in litigation but because his representative let him down. And while I will take that factor into account, for the reasons given at §§33-37 above, it is not normally a factor for leniency."

Summary

1. We are facing an increase in the number of litigants in person.

2. There is a general duty on tribunals to assist litigants, depending on the circumstances, but it is for the tribunal to decide what this duty requires in any particular case and how best to fulfil it, whilst remaining impartial;

3. The fact that a litigant is acting in person is not in itself a reason to disapply procedural rules or orders or directions, or excuse non-compliance with them.

4. The granting of a special indulgence to a litigant in person may be justified where a rule is hard to find or it is difficult to understand, or it is ambiguous;

5. There may be some leeway given to a litigant in person at the margins when the court is considering relief from sanctions or promptness in applying to set aside an order.

6. A litigant in person cannot obtain relief by blaming any default upon their legal representative.

7. When dealing with a litigant in person's application for relief from sanction it is best to focus on the points set out above and to stress that the rule or order is simple to understand or was explained fully to the litigant in person.

8. On the other side of the coin, if you are a litigant in person applying for relief, stress how complicated and obscure the rule or order is that you have breached.

CHAPTER FIVE SETTING ASIDE JUDGMENT

"*it is a custom*
More honor'd in the breach than the observance."
- Hamlet Act 1, scene 4, 7–16

Some litigators are not aware that the rule regarding relief from sanction also applies when applying to set aside judgment. To quote Mr Justice Coulson "there is no greater sanction than judgment being entered in default of a defence, and no more important relief from sanction than being able to set aside that judgment".

It has been held that CPR 3.9 is relevant to any application under CPR 13.3. Before setting aside judgment, the Court needs to first have regard to CPR 13.3 and then if the applicant satisfies those requirements the Court should then consider the three-stage "Denton Test".

Also, when considering promptness under CPR 13.3(2), it has been held that it is artificial to only consider the time between judgment being entered and judgment being set aside, regard should be given to the wider period between the last day a defence could have been filed and that date a draft defence was filed.

Accordingly, it is now more difficult for those seeking to set aside a default judgment to succeed as they are also applying for relief from sanction. This does make sense as in these cases, the Defendant has missed the deadline to file a defence or acknowledgement of service.

Gentry v. Miller and UK Insurance Limited [2016] EWCA Civ 141

In this case, the Court of Appeal considered the approach to applications for relief from sanctions and setting aside a judgement in default in a case where the defaulting party delayed in applying for relief, but was alleging that the claim was fraudulent.

On 17 March 2013 the Claimant and Defendant driver collided. The Claimant's vehicle was written off. Storage and credit hire charges began to accrue. Portal proceedings were issued. On 02 April the Defendant Insurer admitted liability and paid Stage 1 costs. On 08 April the Claimant sent the Insurers a letter asking for PAV of £16,000 and drawing attention to hire charges. Numerous chasers followed. The insurers effectively did nothing, though did on 02 July query the Claimant's notice of intention to issue proceedings.

On 03 July proceedings were issued and served on the Defendant driver only. On 08 August judgment in default of acknowledgment of service was obtained. In late August the insurers voluntarily paid £14,000 and made a part 36 offer in respect of general damages. On 26 September, following application by the Claimant for an interim payment, the Defendant was ordered to pay a further £2,000 damages plus costs, which Insurers duly paid on 15 October.

On 17 October, at a disposal hearing, the Claimant was awarded £75,089 and costs of £12,945. The Defendant driver did not attend.

Having been sent the disposal order, the insurers instructed solicitors.

A number of applications were made. On 25 November Solicitors, then for the Defendant driver, filed a 13.3 application to set aside the judgment in default. On 10 February 2014 they made a further application to cease to act for the Defendant driver and join in insurers. Fraud was alleged between the Claimant and Defendant driver. On 26 February, UKI, now Second Defendant having been joined as a party, applied under 13.3 to set aside the default judgment of 08 August 2013 and under 39.3 to set aside the damages order of 26 September 2013.

Insurers were successful, before a district then circuit judge. The matter came before the Court of Appeal.

Allowing the Claimant's second appeal, the court dismissed the insurer's applications for relief. Cases where fraud is alleged are not exempt from the application of the rules and the test in Mitchell and Denton. A default judgement will not be set aside as a matter of course because a claim is potentially fraudulent.

Going through the Denton guidance, it was accepted that the breach was serious or significant, there was some excuse for the failure to act but there was inexcusable delay in making the applications.

The applications failed the last stage in Denton. When considering all the circumstances of the case and the factors in CPR 3.9(1)(a) and (b), Vos LJ indicated that insurers, as professional litigants, "are in a particularly good position to conduct litigation efficiently and proportionately and to comply with rules and orders". The fact that the insurer was not a party to the claim was no excuse, the insurer should have taken positive steps to protect its interests from the moment it admitted liability.

Vos LJ, remarked that the decision 'may seem harsh' but explained that:

> *"Mitchell and Denton represented a turning point in the need for litigation to be undertaken efficiently and at proportionate cost, and for the rules and orders of the court to be obeyed" and insurers, as professional litigants, were "particularly qualified to respect this change and must do so".*

The Court of Appeal considered the correct approach on applications to set aside where fraud is alleged. The decision is clear: There must be finality in litigation and rules must be obeyed. A default judgment cannot be set aside as a matter of course just because an arguable fraud is alleged long after judgment. The Court of Appeal held it could not "ignore that insurers are professional litigants, who can properly be held responsible for any blatant disregard for their own commercial interests"

> *"Allegations of fraud may in some cases excuse an insurer from taking steps to protect itself, but here this insurer missed every opportunity to do so. It admitted liability before satisfying itself that the claim was*

genuine, perhaps because it mistakenly thought the claim was a small one. That does not excuse the months of delay that then followed. The insurer must in these circumstances face the consequences of its own actions."

This serves as a reminder of the importance of acting promptly in an application for relief from sanctions and an application to set aside judgment. In particular the Court appears to set more store by finality in litigation as opposed to preventing fraud. The Court appears to take a firm line against inefficiency by insurers who are expected to nail their colours to the mast quickly and not change their minds at a later date about the genuineness of a claim.

It is not clear how this sits with the decision in Hayward v Zurich and the principle that fraud unravels all. In that case, the Supreme Court has paved the way for personal injury settlements to be successfully challenged if the claimant is subsequently found to have lied. Maybe it is a question of degree and if a judgment has been obtained where the evidence of fraud is strong, the Court would set aside the judgment on the basis of "all the circumstances" of the case? As a deputy District Judge I often see applications to set aside judgment where the evidence of fraud is circumstantial or weak and there has been inexplicable delay. In those cases the Respondent has good grounds for arguing that the judgment should stand.

Redbourn Group v Fairgate Development [2017] EWHC 1223 (TCC)

The point was highlighted in this case where the court not only considered the factors set out in CPR 13.3 (essentially, whether the defendant has a real prospect of successfully defending the claim and whether the application to set aside has been made promptly), but also took into account the three-stage test set out in Denton.

Background

The claimant obtained judgment in default against the defendant on the basis of the defendant's delay in serving its defence.

The defence was originally due on 25 January 2017. At the defendant's request for a 28-day extension, the claimant offered an extension to 1 February. The defendant did not accept the offer but applied on 1 February for an extension to 22 February. However, it failed to fix a hearing date for that application or to serve the defence before 22 February. On 23 February the claimant applied for judgment in default, which was entered on 9 March. There was therefore 43 days' delay.

On 14 March, the defendant applied to set aside the default judgment under CPR 13.3.

Decision

Coulson J dismissed the application to set aside. He noted that there had originally been some debate as to whether relief from sanctions was relevant to an application under CPR 13.3. However, it had since become clear, following Gentry v Miller [2016] EWCA Civ 141 that it did.

Accordingly, on an application to set aside default judgment, the court must consider the three-stage test set out in Denton after considering the elements set out in CPR 13.3.

Here, on the basis of CPR 13.3, the court concluded that it should not set aside the judgment in default. The defendant had no realistic prospect of defending the claim, and had not acted promptly after judgment was entered, in particular because they had not attached the draft defence and counterclaim to their application to set aside. The draft was not provided until a week before the hearing.

In case the judge was wrong on either of the two elements under CPR 13.3, he went on to address the Denton test.

Here Coulson J was satisfied that the failure in allowing judgment in default to be entered was serious, there was no explanation at all for the failure, and a consideration of all the circumstances of the case (including the defendant's repeated failure to provide information it had promised to the claimant) also led to a conclusion adverse to the defendant.

Accordingly, even if the judge was wrong in his assessment under CPR 13.3, he would have concluded that relief from sanctions should be refused and so the application to set aside would still have failed.

ADVA Optical Networking v Rotronic Instruments [2017] EWHC 1813 (TCC)

In this case, it was set out that even where default judgment has not been entered, a defendant who wishes to file a defence or acknowledgement will need to meet the Denton test.

The Defendant failed to file their Defence on time and made an Application to file their Defence out of time (judgment was not entered). Mr Justice Coulson confirmed that the Denton Test was still to be overcome for the Defendant to have permission to serve their Defence late. Failing to file the Defence on time was deemed serious and there was no good reason for the same. Nevertheless, the Defendant was permitted to serve their Defence for two reasons. First, while the Defence was three months late, there was no real impact on the course of the proceedings. Secondly, the claim against the Defendant was contingent on a second set of ongoing pleadings. Any judgement in default (which disallowing the Defendant to file a Defence would amount to) would effectively be contingent on a separate claim.

Background

The defendant was due to file an acknowledgement of service or defence by 24 March 2017. No default judgment was entered, but at a CMC held on 16 June the court (Carr J) ordered that if the defendant wanted relief from sanctions it had to issue its application no later than 23 June. (The claim was related to a separate set of proceedings, and the CMC was held in respect of both actions.)

On the last day, 23 June, the defendant applied for an extension of time for service and/or relief from sanctions.

Decision

The Judge said there had been some suggestion that the defendant did not require relief at all, but that had rightly not been pursued. He added:

> *"The correct approach is that a retrospective application for an extension of time to serve or file a document should be dealt with on the same principles as a claim for relief from sanctions."*

However, he granted relief from sanctions on the unusual facts of this case, saying this was one of those "relatively rare" cases of serious default where it was appropriate to grant relief.

Although he was satisfied that the breach was serious and there was no good reason for it, the third stage of the test led him to conclude that he should grant relief. This was in particular because (i) the delay had not had any real effect on the course of the proceedings because of amendments that had been made in the related proceedings, and (ii) the claim against the defendant was contingent, and would only give rise to liability if the claimant was found liable in the related proceedings (contrary to its case in those proceedings).. The judge said he was uncomfortable about a situation where the defendant would be made the subject of a judgment which, as things stood, the claimant did not need and which was contrary to its primary case.

Phonographic Performance Ltd v Balgun (t/a Mama Africa) [2018] EWHC 1327 (Ch)

One of the questions in this appeal, was whether relief from sanctions applies when an order for summary judgment has been made as a result of the Defendant not turning up, and whether this constitutes a "trial" within the meaning of CPR 39.3 (5).

The judge held that when a party seeks to set aside an order for summary judgment the Court has to have regard to the provisions of CPR 39.3(5) but is not bound by them and that strictly speaking the principles relating to relief of sanctions are not relevant to an application to set aside an order for summary judgment, but the Court has to take them into account anyway.

The claimant in this case brought an action for breach of copyright on the basis that the defendant was infringing copyright. The defendant did not attend the application because he was at another on the same day. Judgment was given in September 2017, but it was not until November 2017 that the defendant made an application to set aside the judgment.

The Master refused the application and the defendant appealed.
On appeal the judge considered the relevant criteria when seeking to set aside the order for summary judgment.

CPR 39.3(5) provides that:

> *"Where an application is made under para.(2) or (3) by a party who failed to attend the trial, the court may grant the application only if the applicant-*
>
> *(a) has acted promptly when he found out that the court had exercised its power to strike out or to enter judgment or make an order against him;*
>
> *(b) had good reason for not attending the trial; and*

(c) has a reasonable prospect of success at the trial."

The Master concluded that the defendant had not acted promptly and he doubted the credibility of the defendant's explanation that he had difficulty with the post. He considered that the defendant did not have a good explanation for not attending the hearing on 20 September as he had notice of it. The Master considered that the defendant did not have a defence to the claim.

In the application for permission to appeal, the Defendant argued that he was not aware of any proceedings against him, that he acted promptly when he became aware of the judgment and applied to set it aside and that there was a real prospect of successfully defending the claim.

The argument on the application for permission to appeal was that the Master's approach to the principles applicable to setting aside an order for summary judgment obtained in the absence of a party was wrong, in that the test for setting aside judgment after a trial was not the right approach.

The Court agreed that summary judgment hearings do not amount to a trial, but the principles of CPR Part 3.9 are still applicable.

The Judge quoted practice direction to CPR 24 provides in para.8.1:

> *"If an order for summary judgment is made against a respondent who does not appear at the hearing of the application, the respondent may apply for the order to be set aside or varied. (see also rule23.11)*
>
> *8.2 On the hearing of an application under para.8.1 the court may make such order as it thinks fit."*

Tubelike Limited (In Liquidation) & Others -v- Visitjourneys.com Limited [2016] EWHC 43 (Ch)

In this case Chief Master Marsh considered this provision. As he pointed out, there is no guidance in The White Book as to how this provision should be applied and, indeed, it is not part of the rules. The reference to CPR 23.11 is not helpful in that that rule provides that a court may relist an application where a party has not turned up. He was referred to CPR 39.35 as well as the law on relief from sanctions and other provisions of the CPR where judgments can be set aside and he concluded (at para.22 of his judgment):

> *"I consider that the right approach for the court to adopt when considering an application to set aside judgment made under rule24 in the absence of a party is to apply by analogy the provisions of rule.39.3(5) without being a slave to the requirements of that rule. The power contained in para.8.1 of Practice Direction 24 gives an unfettered jurisdiction to the court and in exercising that power the court should have in mind the criteria in rule39.3(5) and also the provisions of the overriding objective. I am not persuaded by Ms. Helmore's submission that I should have regard to rule 3.6 and therefore, the provisions for relief against sanctions contained in rule 3.9. To do so, would be to heavily overload the approach the court should adopt to criteria which are foreign to it."*

In the appeal in Phonographic Performance, it was submitted that this is not the right approach to setting aside summary judgment orders because CPR 39.3(5) is directed towards a situation where the court is concerned to ensure finality after a trial.

However, the judge considered that as Chief Master Marsh made clear in Tubelike, he was only adopting the CPR 39. 3(5) requirements as a guide and it seemed to her that they ought not to be too rigidly applied in circumstances where there has not been a trial, and that the court should also take into account other rules of the CPR which provide that judgments can be set aside, for example, judgments in default under CPR 13.

The judge therefore found that:

> *"it is not inappropriate for a court to take into account the considerations that are set out in CPR 39. 3(5). The promptness with which a party has acted, the reasons for non-appearance and whether the party applying has real prospects of succeeding if the matter were to get to trial are all relevant considerations. There may be others, including whether there are other reasons why the matter ought to be tried.*
>
> *I agree with Master Marsh, and nobody has urged me to do otherwise, that the learning on relief from sanctions is not helpful in this context.*
>
> *Master Price had the Tubelike case before him and he did use the conditions in CPR 39. 3(5) as a guide but it is hard to say that those considerations were not relevant ones for the court to take into account in exercising its jurisdiction, provided that they were not applied with undue rigidity. Therefore, attractively as the submission was put, I do not consider that Master Price' decision can be criticised as wrong on the basis of the approach he took to the exercise of his discretion."*
>
> *"The Judge then looked at whether the Defendant had acted promptly and found that the Master had not been wrong to exercise his discretion in the way that he did. "First of all, it is said that he was wrong to say that the defendant did not act promptly. It is clear that the order was served on the defendant the day after it was made. It also appears that he did contact the court in October, but he took no steps until enforcement was attempted in November. While another judge may have taken a different view as to whether this was sufficiently prompt or not, bearing in mind that the defendant was acting in person I do not consider that Master Price can be criticised for finding that the application had not been made promptly. It was a view he was entitled to take."*

> "*On the question of the reason why the defendant failed to attend the hearing, I consider that Master Price was right to conclude that the defendant had proper notice and the notes to CPR 39.3(5) in The White Book state that a mere assertion that a party was unaware of the hearing date is unlikely to be sufficient. The defendant knew of the proceedings (he filed a defence and corresponded with the claimant) and the attempts made by the claimant to bring the hearing of the summary judgment application to his attention make it unlikely that he did not know of it.*"

> "*However, what the Master perhaps did not take sufficient notice of was that the defendant was engaged in a hearing of other proceedings on the date when the summary judgment application was heard. The defendant clearly mentioned this a couple of times to the Master and he does not mention it in his judgment. However, it is not clear to me why the defendant did not inform he court in advance that he could not attend on the date fixed for the summary judgment application.*"

The judge went on to find that the defendant had no defence on the merits. The application for permission to was refused.

By analogy with applications to set aside default judgments where relief from sanctions is taken into account, the three-stage test and CPR 3.9 is taken into account when applying to set aside an order for summary judgment.

ITPE v Franks [2018] EWHC 1765 (QB)

In this case, where a defendant sought to set aside judgment, it was decided on appeal that the relief from sanctions principles are required to be considered after the issue of setting aside a default judgment.

The claimant was suing the defendant for a rape that took place in 1996.

A letter of claim was sent to the defendant in prison in May 2017. The claim was issued (and the claimant granted anonymity) in June 2017.

The claim was served on the defendant, in prison, on the 1st August 2017. No acknowledgement or defence was received. judgment was entered on the 24th August.

On the 21st September 2017 the claimant's solicitors wrote asking for an interim payment on account of damages and costs.

On the 5th October the defendant made an application to set aside judgment and relief from sanctions for failure to file or serve an acknowledgment of service.

On the 1st November 2017 the defendant filed and served a costs budget and made an application for relief from sanctions for failing to serve it on time.

The judge summarised the position before the Master.

The Appellant had applied to set aside the default judgment on the grounds that he had a real prospect of defending the claim on limitation grounds. This was on the straightforward basis that the tort had been committed in 1997/8, the claim had not been issued until 2017, and so it was out of time under s 11 of the 1980 Act.

The judge allowed the appeal. He held that the Master had adopted the wrong approach to the question of setting aside a default judgment:

> "*The approach which the Master should have adopted in relation to the application to set aside the default judgment is that set out in the judgment of Christopher Clarke LJ in Regione Piemonte v Dexia Crediop SpA [2014] EWCA Civ 1298, paras 38-41, which was approved in Gentry v Miller [2016] 1 WLR 2696, paras 23-24. In the former case, Christopher Clarke LJ said:*

"38. A question arose at the hearing of the appeal as to the extent to which the principles laid down in Mitchell v News Group Newspapers Ltd [2014] 1 WLR 795 applied to applications to set aside a default judgement. Since the hearing this Court has given judgment in Denton v TH White Ltd [2014] EWCA Civ 906 and the parties have made written submissions on it. Neither case was concerned with applications to set aside a judgment.

39. In essence Piedmont submits that the Mitchell/Denton principles do not apply to an application to set aside a default judgment. The majority in Denton considered that the Mitchell decision was correct to attribute a particular importance to the factors listed at CPR 3.9 (1) (a) (the need "for litigation to be conducted efficiently and at proportionate cost") and (b) (the need "to enforce compliance with rules, practice directions and orders") because the Civil Procedure Rule Committee had rejected a recommendation in the Review of Civil Litigation Costs Final Report that CPR 3.9.1 should be reworded so that 3.9.1 (b) read "the interests of justice in the particular case". But the Final Report did not propose any amendment to CPR 13.3 so that the reasoning of the majority in Denton does not apply to it. There is thus, it is submitted, no reason to conclude that the Mitchell/Denton principles apply to an application under CPR 13.3 or that promptness under CPR 13.3 should be regarded as anything more than a factor. I disagree.

*40. **In my judgment the matter stands thus. CPR 13.3 requires an applicant to show that he has real prospects of a successful defence or some other good reason to set the judgement aside. If he does, the court's discretion is to be exercised in the light of all the circumstances and the overriding objective. The Court must have regard to all the factors it considers relevant of which promptness is both a mandatory and an important consideration. Since the overriding objective of the Rules is to enable the court to deal with cases justly and at proportionate cost, and since under the new CPR 1.1 (2) (f) the latter includes enforcing compliance with rules, practice directions and orders,** the considerations set out in CPR 3.9 are to be taken into account: see Hussein v Birmingham*

> *City Council [2005] EWCA Civ 1570 per Chadwick LJ at [30]; Mid-East Sales v United Engineering and Trading Co (PVT) Ltd [2014] EWHC 1457 at [85]. So also is the approach to CPR 3.9 in Mitchell/Denton. The fact that the Court's judgment in Denton was reinforced by the fact that CPR 3.9 was not reworded in the manner proposed by Jackson LJ does not detract from the relevance of CPR 3.9, and what was said about it in Denton, to applications under CPR 13.*
>
> *41. Denton makes clear that any application for relief against sanctions involves considering (i) the seriousness and significance of the default (ii) the reason for it and (iii) all the circumstances of the case. At the third stage factors (a) and (b) in CPR 3.9 are of particular, but not paramount, importance."*

The judge decided that the Master had got it the wrong way round, saying that:

> "*As the case law I have quoted makes clear,* ***the Master should first have considered the merits of the Appellant's claim that there was a real prospect of succeeding in a defence and, if she was in the Appellant's favour on that issue, then gone on to consider how to exercise her discretion in light of her conclusion on promptness and the other factors identified by Christopher Clarke LJ. In saying this, I do not intend to be critical of the Master. She was not assisted by the way in which the advocates presented the issues to her. It does not appear that she was shown the relevant authorities, although Denton was referred to in passing.***
>
> ***However, had she adopted the correct approach, in my judgment the Master would have been bound to conclude that if there was a real prospect of the Appellant defending the claim, then her discretion should be exercised in the Appellant's favour to set aside the default judgment.*** "

It follows from this case that in applications to set aside judgment the primary consideration should be the applicable rule and the Denton Test is subsidiary to that.

Summary

- When applying to set aside judgment, it is important to consider relief from sanction also
- Deal with Claim Forms immediately and don't allow judgment to be entered
- Promptness relates not just to the time after judgment and before the application but the time that has lapsed since judgment being entered.
- The defendant needs to offer an explanation as to:
    - How judgment came to be entered in default.
    - Any delays between issue and judgment being instructed. In Redbourn the judge noted:

      "*analogy can be drawn with the recent trend in cases concerned with late amendments, such as Su-Ling v Goldman Sachs International [2015] EWHC 759 (Comm), where Carr J made plain that, on the recent authorities, the absence of a proper explanation for delay will often, without more, lead to the application to amend being refused.*"
- Exhibit a draft defence to show that "the defendant has a real prospect of successfully defending the claim". This has to be established by evidence. This is best done by first-hand evidence not second-hand evidence from the solicitor.

- Set out the case fully when the application is first made. Further evidence put in shortly before the hearing may contribute to a lack of promptness.

- In Goldcrest Distribution Ltd -v- McCole [2016] EWHC 1571 (Ch) (in relation to setting aside judgment on a counterclaim) The Judge said:

  "It is ordinarily not right to serve an application notice for such an important order as this with some evidence in support at the time, and then, several weeks later, have a second bite at the cherry with an additional witness statement."

- Demonstrate that there is a real prospect of successfully defending the claim

- There is no point arguing that allowing a default judgment to be entered is not serious or significant, or that there is a good reason for doing so. However, the failure to give an explanation at all is likely to be fatal.

- All the circumstances of the case may be the key part of the test. There is nothing more acutely embarrassing for a claimant than to have judgment in default entered on a counterclaim.

- In relation to claimants it is essential that counterclaims are identified at once and the need to file a defence to counterclaim dealt with. Remember that there is no acknowledgment of service stage. The Defence to Counterclaim must be served within 14 days of service of the Counterclaim (20.3.3). A full and detailed Defence to the points made in the Counterclaim is required.

- If fraud is suspected, apply quickly and provide clear evidence of the fraud.

- An application to set aside judgment is far more difficult than previously.

CHAPTER SIX
SERVICE OF CLAIM FORM

One rule that Solicitors frequently fall foul of, with potentially catastrophic results, is that requiring the Claim Form to be served within 4 months. If they do fail to serve in time, the rules on relief from sanction do not apply, as applications are made under CPR Rule 7.6. However, there is a similarity of approach as set out in Hashtroodi v Hancock [2004] EWCA Civ 652. This chapter is included for the sake of completeness in case the reader assumes that late service of a Claim Form is covered by CPR 3.9.

The case of Haley v Siddiqui [2014] EWHC 835 is authority for the proposition that an application is not an application for relief from sanctions.

CPR Rule 7.5 provides that a Claim Form must be served by 12.00 midnight on the calendar day four months after the date of service.

And "(2) Where the claim form is to be served out of the jurisdiction, the claim form must be served in accordance with Section IV of Part 6 within 6 months of the date of issue."

CPR 7.6, dealing with the extension of time, provides:

> "*Extension of time for serving a claim form*
>
> *7.6-(1) The claimant may apply for an order extending the period for compliance with rule 7.5.*
>
> *(2) The general rule is that an application to extend the time for compliance with rule 7.5 must be made-*
>
> *(a) within the period specified by rule 7.5; or*

(b) where an order has been made under this rule, within the period for service specified by that order.

(3) If the claimant applies for an order to extend the time for compliance after the end of the period specified by rule 7.5 or by an order made under this rule, the court may make such an order only if-

(a) the court has failed to serve the claim form; or

(b) the claimant has taken all reasonable steps to comply with rule 7.5 but has been unable to do so; and

(c) in either case, the claimant has acted promptly in making the application.

(4) An application for an order extending the time for compliance with rule 7.5 –

(a) must be supported by evidence; and

(b) may be made without notice."

A solicitor's incompetence is unlikely to be grounds upon which to obtain an extension, following Hashtroodi v Hancock.

Parties can agree to extend time for service, as they often do in order to obtain further medical evidence for example. It is not one of the steps precluded by CPR 2.11.

If a party fails to serve Particulars of Claim, they can apply for an extension and adopt the relief from sanction process.

There is no bar to re issuing if a Claim Form is not served on time, except if a limitation period applies, but if there has been more than mere negligent failure, the Defendant may argue abuse of process.

Foran -v- Secret Surgery Ltd [2016] EWHC 1029 (QB)

The decision in this case demonstrates the risks of a claimant not serving the Claim Form timeously.

The claimant was bringing an action for clinical negligence against a number of defendants, three of which were domiciled in abroad. Proceedings were issued on the 6th May 2015 and served on the first defendant (who was domiciled in England) on the 2nd September 2015.

The claimant had six months to serve the 2nd – 4th defendants, which took them to the 6th November 2015. On the 29th October 2015 the claimant issued a without notice application for an extension of time. On the 9th November 2015 Master Roberts made an order extending time for Service.

The Order was not served on the defendants, and it was only served the day before the hearing of the appeal. At the hearing that took place on the 11th January 2016 neither advocate attending was aware that the order had been made.

The hearing that took place on the 11th January 2016 was on notice. The Master found that the claimant had taken reasonable steps to serve the 2nd – 4th defendants and granted an extension of time for service.

The Appeal

The legal principles governing the Court's approach to an application under CPR 7.6(2) are found in the judgments of the Court of Appeal in Hashtroodi v Hancock [2004] EWCA Civ 652; Collier v Williams [2006] EWCA Civ 20 and Bayat v Cecil [2011] EWCA Civ 135.

In Hashtroodi the Court noted the striking contrast between CPR 7.6(2) and the preconditions in 7.6(3), which showed that it was not intended to impose any threshold condition on the right to apply for an extension of time under CPR 7.6(2). The discretion should therefore be exercised having regard to the overriding objective. Nevertheless, in exercising that discretion the Court said as follows at paragraphs 18 – 20:

> "*18. … We have no doubt what it will always be relevant for the court to determine and evaluate the reason why the claimant did not serve the claim form within the specified period. This has nothing to do with the fact that under the former procedural code, the threshold requirement was that the plaintiff should show good reason. It is because the overriding objective is that of enabling the court to deal with cases 'justly', and it is not possible to deal with an application for an extension of time under CPR 7.6(2) justly without knowing why the claimant has failed to serve the claim form within the specified period. As a matter of commonsense, the court will always want to know why the claim form was not served within the specified period. As Mr Zuckerman says at para 4.121 [Adrian Zuckerman: Civil Procedure] …*
>
> '*For it is only fair to ask whether the applicant is seeking the court's help to overcome a genuine problem that he has encountered in carrying out service or whether he is seeking relief from the consequences of his own neglect. A claimant who has experienced difficulty should normally be entitled to the court's help, but an applicant who has merely left service too late is not entitled to as much consideration. Whether the limitation period has expired is also of considerable importance. If an extension is sought beyond four months after the expiry of the limitation period, the claimant is effectively asking the court to disturb a defendant who is by now entitled to assume that his rights can no longer be disputed.*"
>
> "*19. Whereas under the previous law, a plaintiff who was unable to show a good reason for not serving in time failed at the threshold, under the CPR, a more calibrated approach is to be adopted. If there is a very good reason for the failure to serve the claim form within the specified period, then an extension of time will usually be granted. Thus, where the court has been unable to serve the claim form or the claimant has taken all reasonable steps to serve the claim form, but*

has been unable to do so (the CPR 7.6(3) conditions), the court will have no difficulty in deciding that there is a very good reason for the failure to serve. The weaker the reason, the more likely the court will be to refuse to grant the extension.

20. If the reason why the claimant has not served the claim form within the specified period is that he (or his legal representative) simply overlooked the matter, that will be a strong reason for the court refusing to grant an extension of time for service. One of the important aims of the Woolf reforms was to introduce more discipline into the conduct of civil litigation. One of the ways of achieving this is to insist that time limits be adhered to unless there is good reason for a departure. In Biguzzi, Lord Woolf a said at p 1933D:

'If the court were to ignore delays which occur, then undoubtedly there will be a return to the previous culture of regarding time limits as being unimportant.'"

In the context of a three-year limitation period for personal injury claims the Court noted that the time limits in CPR 7.5. were already generous. Moreover they pointed out (at para 21) that "… the claim form does not have to contain full details of the claim. All that is required is a concise statement of the nature of the claim: see CPR 16.2(1)(a)."

The Court ruled that there was no reason in that case for the failure to serve in time other than the incompetence of the claimant's solicitors, which was said to be "… a powerful reason for refusing to grant an extension of time." The solicitors' failures were found to be "particularly egregious" and the Court was in no doubt that there should not be an extension of time for service of the claim form.

Collier

In Collier the Court heard a number of conjoined appeals, in which one of the questions to be decided was whether the guidance given in

Hashtroodi was being properly applied. The Court repeated (at para 87) the relevance of the CPR 7.6(3) requirements to the exercise of the discretion under 7.6(2):

> "*87. When deciding whether to grant an extension of time under CPR 7.6(2), the court is required to consider how good a reason there was for the failure to serve in time (assuming that the application is dealt with after the end of the 4 months period): the stronger the reason, the more likely the court will be to extend time; and the weaker the reason, the less likely. This involves making a judgment about the reason why service has not been effected within the 4 months period. It is a more subtle exercise than that required under CPR 7.6(3) which provides that unless all reasonable steps have been taken, the court cannot extend time.*"

They emphasised in other passages (see paras 100 and 131) that service of the claim form is "a crucial step in the proceedings", the rules being designed to ensure that so far as possible the claim form is brought to the attention of the Defendant and, where he is represented, his legal representatives. The critical task for the Court in these cases is "to determine and evaluate the reason why the Claimant did not serve the claim form within the specified period." Awaiting receipt of an accountant's report was held not to be a good reason for delaying service of the claim form, as opposed to service of the particulars of claim, for which a separate application should be made to the Court.

Hoddinott

In Hoddinott v Persimmon Homes (Wessex) Ltd [2007] EWCA Civ 1203, the Court of Appeal explained the importance of service of the claim form in these terms at paragraphs 54 – 55:

> "*54. … But service of the claim form serves three purposes. The first is to notify the defendant that the claimant has embarked on the formal process of litigation and to inform him of the nature of the claim. The second is to enable the defendant to participate in the*

process and have some say in the way in which the claim is prosecuted: until he has been served, the defendant may know that proceedings are likely to be issued, but he does not know for certain and he can do nothing to move things along. The third is to enable the court to control the litigation process. If extensions of time for serving pleadings or taking other steps are justified, they will be granted by the court. But until the claim form is served, the court has no part to play in the proceedings. A key element of the Woolf reforms was to entrust the court with far more control over proceedings than it had exercised under the previous regime. The rules must be applied so as to give effect to the overriding objective: this includes dealing with a case so as to ensure so far as is practicable that cases are dealt with expeditiously and fairly (CPR 1.1(1)(d)). That is why the court is unlikely to grant and extension of time for service of the claim form under CPR 7.6(2) if no good reason has been shown for the failure to serve within the 4 months' period.

55. Thus, there are good reasons why the court should scrutinise with care applications to grant an extension of time for service of the claim form. …"

Bayat v Cecil

In Bayat v Cecil the Court of Appeal considered CPR 7.6 in the context of a commercial dispute. In a high value contract claim an application for a six-month extension of time for service of the claim form had been made and granted before the four month period had expired, on the basis that the Claimant needed time to secure funding for the claim. During the six month extension granted, during which the limitation period expired, the Claimant applied for and was granted a further six months extension. The Court of Appeal upheld the Defendant's appeal and ruled that the extensions should be set aside.

Sir Stanley Burnton, acknowledging the generous width of the discretion under CPR 7.6(2), referred to the dicta in Hoddinott and held that the Claimants should have served the claim form within the period of its initial validity. If they were in financial difficulties they should have issued an application for a stay, or for an extension of time for the necessary procedural steps to be taken, which would have been matters for case management by the Court after the claim form had been served. It was not for the Claimants unilaterally to decide to postpone the service of the claim form. Hashtroodi was a case in which the Claimant's solicitor had been negligent. In general, an extension of time is not justified where its need is due to the negligence of those acting for the Claimant. However, at paragraph 44 he said that "... it does not follow that an extension is necessarily to be granted in a limitation case where those acting for the Claimant have acted competently."

In relation to limitation Sir Stanley said as follows at paragraphs 48 and 50:

> "*48. CPR r 7.6(3) differs from CPR r 7.6(2) in an important respect. If an application for an extension of time is made after the expiration of the validity of the claim form, the court has no discretion to exercise in favour of the claimant unless, in a case in which the claimant was to serve it, he 'has taken all reasonable steps' to serve within the period of its validity but has been unable to do so. It would to my mind be curious if any different test may be applied to an application for an extension of time made within the period of the validity of the claim form in a case in which the limitation defence of the defendant will be or may be prejudiced. At the very least, even if he has not taken all reasonable steps, the claimant should have to show that he has taken reasonable steps. I refer to what Rix LJ recently said in his judgment in Aktas v Adepta [2010] EWCA Civ 1170 with which the other members of the Court agreed:*
>
> *91. The reason why failure to serve in time has always been dealt with strictly (even if CPR 7.6(3) represents a still further tightening of the rules where a retrospective request for an extension is made out of time) is in my judgment bound up with the fact that in England, unlike (all or most) civil law jurisdictions, proceedings are commenced when issued and not when served. However, it is not until service that a defendant has been given proper notice of the pro-*

ceedings in question. Therefore, the additional time between issue and service is, in a way, an extension of the limitation period. A claimant can issue proceedings on the last day of the limitation period and can still, whatever risks he takes in doing so, enjoy a further four month period until service, and his proceedings will still be in time. In such a system, it is important therefore that the courts strictly regulate the period granted for service. If it were otherwise, the statutory limitation period could be made elastic at the whim or sloppiness of the claimant or his solicitors. For the same reason, the argument that if late service were not permitted, the claimant would lose his claim, because it would become time barred, becomes a barren excuse. But even where the claimant is well within the limitation period despite his delay in serving, there is a clear public interest in the rules and the courts curtailing the efficacy of a claim form which, because it has not been served, is not very different from an unposted letter. Therefore, the strictness with which the time for service is supervised has entirely valid public interest underpinnings which are quite separate from the doctrine of abuse of process. It is sufficient for the rules to provide for service within a specified time and for the courts to require claimants to adhere strictly to that time limit or else timeously provide a good reason for some dispensation.

…

50. Hoddinott is authority for the proposition that the court may grant an extension of time under CPR r 7.6(2) even where there is no good reason for failing to serve in the period of validity of the claim form. However, it was a case in which there was no question of a limitation defence being prejudiced by the extension: as remarked in paragraph 54 of the judgment, the claimant could have issued a new claim form. It was also a case in which the defendant had been made aware of the proceedings, since it had been sent a copy of the claim form. It required those two facts to justify the extension granted by the Court of Appeal. Neither was applicable in the present case."

The Judge below was criticised in that case for not weighing in the balance the Defendant's loss of their limitation defence. While the extension in question was only just outside the extended period, Sir Stanley observed (paras 54-55) that "... in the law of limitation, a miss is as good as a mile. Furthermore, the primary question in a case where limitation is engaged is ... whether, if an extension of time is granted, the Defendant will or may be deprived of a limitation defence." While it is relevant "... that the effect of a refusal to extend time for service of the claim form will deprive the Claimant of what may be a good claim ... the stronger the claim, more important is the defendant's limitation defence, which should not be circumvented by an extension of time for serving a claim form save in exceptional circumstances."

Rix LJ, agreeing with his judgment, observed that the strictness with which the jurisdiction to extend time is viewed is of general application. On the facts of the case, posing the question whether the Claimant's reason for wanting successive extensions of time could be said to be a good reason, he concluded as follows:

> *"91. ... Since a limitation period expired in November 2008, during the period of the first extension (from September 2008 to March 2009), an especially good reason would, in my judgment, on Dyson LJ's calibrated approach, be required. The reports are not replete with examples, at any rate where the claimant has not established a real problem in carrying out service."*

Foran

In Foran, the Court found that the guidance provided by the Court of Appeal is clearly of general application; and that the factors being relied upon by the appellant were, either inadequately explained in evidence, or omitted altogether. When the Court is considering whether to grant an extension of time under CPR 7.6(2) each case will naturally turn on its own facts, but those facts must be properly evidenced and carefully scrutinised.

The Court ruled that the time limits within the CPR, having the legitimate aim of the good administration of justice, should always be adhered to unless there is good reason. Service of the claim form is an important step in litigation, in particular in cases where there is a potential limitation defence. The six-month period allowed for service out of the jurisdiction seemed to the judge to be a generous provision.

The judge considered that applications under CPR 7.6(2) for an extension of time and the evidence provided in support should therefore be scrutinised with care. Practice Direction 7A provides, at paragraph 8, that the evidence filed in support should state all the circumstances relied on, and provide a full explanation as to why the claim has not been served.

In a case where the limitation period expired almost six months before the application for an extension of time was made, the Court considered that the evidence failed that test. The statement contained a far from full explanation of the reasons for the delay in this case.

The statement was brief and no relevant correspondence or other documentary evidence was exhibited to it. The timetable of events was set out but insufficient explanation was provided as to how that timetable demonstrated a good reason for the delays that are manifest on an analysis of its contents. The matters described by the Master in paragraphs 16 – 17 of his judgment as amounting to valid reasons for an extension of time, merely recited the timetable without further analysis or evaluation of what seem to be some obvious omissions. It was no answer to say that the case was unusual and complex due to the foreign element and associated factors, because it was those same factors that necessitated a more urgent approach to addressing the likely problems with service out of the jurisdiction than was evidenced in the statement.

The judge rejected without hesitation any suggestion that there was wilful disregard of the rules by the Claimant's solicitors, or that there was a deliberate flouting of the rules. Ultimately the question for the Master was whether a good reason had been shown on the evidence before him for granting the extension of time. In the Court's judgment the evidence provided in support of the application fell short of what was required to permit a finding in the Claimant's favour.

If, as it appears, an active decision was taken by the solicitors not to serve the claim form on any Defendant until a medical report was available, that would not in any event amount to a good reason for failing to serve the claim form in time (see Collier above). It was submitted, although there is no evidence about it, that it was probably considered to be more helpful to the Defendants for them to have detailed particulars of claim and supporting documents served along with the claim form all in one go. On the authorities, however, that is not a satisfactory reason for failure to serve the claim form. Problems with experts and delay in providing the medical report should be the subject of separate application to the Court for case management directions, if necessary, subsequent to service of the claim form.

Further, the Court accepted the submission that the Master did not address and weigh in the balance the loss to the Defendants of their potential limitation defence in this case. There is no dispute that he erred in stating that the application for an extension of time in this case was made within the limitation period.

For all these reasons the Judge ruled that the Master's decision was wrong and cannot stand. The Defendants' appeal was therefore allowed.

Don't take advantage

Abbott -v-Econowall Ltd [2016] EWHC 660 (IPEC)

In Abbott -v-Econowall Ltd [2016] EWHC 660 (IPEC) The Judge made some important observations about the conduct expected in litigation. It also contains some important lessons in relation to agreeing extensions of time for service.

The claimants issued proceedings alleging infringement of a patent.

The claim form was not served until after the expiry of the date for service as extended by agreement. Also the statement of truth on the claim form was not signed.

The defendant sought an order disputing the jurisdiction on the grounds that the claim form was not served in time.

Alternatively the defendant sought an order striking out the action because the claim was not served in time.

By way of response the claimant served:

- An order that service of a photocopy of the unsigned claim form just after issue was good service.
- An order under CPR 3.9 granting relief from sanction.
- An order retrospectively extending the time for service of the claim form to the date it was sent.

The defendants agreed an extension of time for service of the claim form. However there was some ambiguity in the extension.

The party mis-read the letter from the defendants' solicitors. The judge stated that:

> "*To begin with, parties to litigation are plainly not obliged to inform the opposing side of its mistakes – in the sense of steps taken or positions adopted which appear not to be in that other side's best interest. Each side must look after itself. However this is subject to parties never losing sight of the overriding objective. It seems to me that this requires parties to take reasonable steps to ensure, so far as is reasonably possible, that there is clear common understanding between them as to the identity of the issues in the litigation and also as to related matters, including procedural arrangements. The reason is that any breakdown in such understanding is likely to lead to wasted expense and also to hamper expedition in the progress of the case, often because it gives rise to an application to the court to sort matters out. This in turn requires allocation of the court's resources which could otherwise be avoided.*

> *"Therefore, in my view, where a litigant becomes aware of a real possibility that a genuine misunderstanding has arisen between the parties regarding a significant matter, the litigant should take reasonable steps to clear it up. Dispelling such misunderstandings is likely to ensure that the litigation will be conducted more efficiently and I see no real likelihood of any consequent unfairness to either side."*

> *"...when agreements (or court orders) about the date by which a thing is to be done are made, it is always better to specify that date precisely rather than by reference to a period such a week or a month. There is always room for misunderstandings or accidentally fixing a weekend or Bank Holiday if time periods are used. Old hands wisely use "On or before the [blank] day of [blank]."*

The Judge disapproved of any parties "playing inappropriate technical games.

Medhi Kohsravi -v- British American Tobacco PLC [2016] EWHC 123 (QB)

In this case, Sir David Eady stated that he would have set aside an order extending time for service of the claim form.

This case highlights the fact that without notice extensions of time are risky because they are liable to be set aside and then the claim fails.

The wisest course of action is to serve and then apply for a stay.

The claimant issued proceedings against the defendant and obtained a without notice orders to extend time for service of the claim form and particulars of claim. The claimant applied for an order striking out the claim, alternatively to set aside the extensions of time. The judge struck the matter out. However, he also considered the issues in relation to an extension of time.

In relation to the application to set aside the extensions of time for service of the claim form and particulars of claim, in this case it was made in reliance upon CPR 11(1) and, as appropriate, within 14 days of the acknowledgement of service. For good measure, alternative applications were also made under CPR 23.10 and 3.1(7).

The judge held that the jurisdiction to extend time under CPR 7.6 must obviously be exercised in accordance with the overriding objective. A good reason must be given: see e.g. Hashtroodi v Hancock [2004] 3 All ER 530 and Hoddinott v Persimmon Homes [2008] 1 WLR 806. While it has naturally been recognised that a litigant can establish a good reason where he has been unable to serve despite his best efforts, it seems clear that the court will not generally recognise mere lack of funding as such a reason: Cecil v Bayat [2011] 1 WLR 3086.

The other basis advanced was that time was needed to gather further evidence. This might have justified the seeking of a stay (at an inter partes hearing) once the proceedings were launched (on the basis of evidence already obtained), but it was hard to see how it would be a reasonable ground for holding up service of the claim form for nearly 18 months.

The judge was invited to err on the side of generosity, having particular regard to the stress and poor health with which the Claimant had to contend with in recent years. On the other hand, the judge felt that:

> *"Defendants too are entitled to consideration and fair treatment in the litigation process. The longer the case is allowed to drag on, the greater the time and expenditure they will have to devote to it (with little prospect of recovering their costs if ultimately successful). They are entitled not only to clarity in the formulation of the claim, but also to be able to see at least the prospect of light at the end of the tunnel. This is especially so where the claim in question depends upon events alleged to have taken place many years ago."*

> *"Sometimes, where a claimant's difficulties can already be seen as attributable to wrongdoing on the part of the defendant (as often*

> *happens in personal injury or clinical negligence cases), it may be appropriate for the court to show a degree of forbearance if the claimant has to overcome hurdles in coping with the litigation in consequence. There may be circumstances in which a defendant should not be permitted to take unfair or tactical advantage of its own wrongdoing. Here, however, there is a fundamental issue as to whether any of this Claimant's problems should be laid at the door of these Defendants at all."*
>
> *"The overriding objective requires that the disciplines imposed by the CPR should not be allowed to lapse unnecessarily. Any delay in the normal timetable must be justified by the applicant. Such extensions should certainly not be granted as a formality or go through "on the nod". The claim form would ordinarily have been due for service on the first Defendant in May 2014, but the extensions meant that the whole process was delayed for over 16 months. Then two more Defendants were added, which would in itself be likely to entail further delay as they acquaint themselves with the facts. All this was against the background of apparent inactivity following the initial letter of 2 August 2012 and especially during the prolonged silence between 30 March 2013 and 27 February 2015 (described in the witness statement of Ruth Grant at paras 14-15). It seems to me, therefore, that the scope for indulgence had become rather limited. Were it not for the orders I propose to make under CPR 3.4 and 24.2, I would therefore have been willing to set aside the extension orders."*

If in doubt, make an inter partes application.

Summary

1. CPR 3.9 has no relevance to applications in relation to extend time for service of the claim form. The three-stage test does not apply but the "good reason" test does apply.

2. When making an application for an extension you must set out the evidence in support in some detail and satisfy the court, by that evidence, that there is a good reason for the failure to serve within the relevant period.

3. Problems serving a defendant domiciled abroad does not, of itself, represent a good reason. The time for service of such a defendant is extended by the rules to six months to allow for such difficulties.

4. It is a serious matter to apply for an extension. "The time limits within the CPR, having the legitimate aim of the good administration of justice, should always be adhered to unless there is good reason. Service of the claim form is an important step in litigation, in particular in cases where there is a potential limitation defence"

5. Always ensure you are clear about any extension period agreed.

6. Difficulties with funding, or formulating the case, are not good reasons for extending time for service.

7. It is always better to serve and seek a stay after service, rather than applying afterwards.

8. It is better to make an on notice application to avoid the risk of an order being set aside.

9. Make any application promptly.

10. Don't take a tactical advantage if you are opposing an extension.

CHAPTER SEVEN
AUTOMATIC STRIKING OUT FOR FAILURE TO PAY TRIAL FEES

We look in this Chapter at non-payment of trial fees and the risk of sanctions if you fail to pay the trial fee on time.

Non-Payment of Trial Fee

People often do not read the orders properly and sanctions can be buried away in the text.

Some of the most common errors include failing to pay the trial or hearing fee, or not applying to the Court before the end of a stay.

In respect of the trial fee, the orders often say:

> "*Unless the Claimant does by 4pm on x date, pay to the Court the trial fee of £x or file a properly completed application (ie one which provides all the required information in the manner requested) for help with fees then the claim will be struck out with effect from x date without further order and unless the Court orders otherwise you will be liable for the costs which the defendant has incurred.*"

The position is clear. If you don't pay the trial fee on time the case will be struck out and it is no excuse to say that the cheque was in the post. The court is likely to treat such an excuse in the same way as a child who claims that the dog ate the homework, subject to the argument set out below.

If the Court makes an order with which you disagree, without a hearing, you generally have 7 days to file an application to set aside or vary. Any longer than that and you will also need to apply for relief.

The Rules

Sanctions for non-payment of the trial fee by the claimant

3.7A1

(1) In this rule and in rule 3.7AA—

(a) "Fees Order 2008" means the Civil Proceedings Fees Order 2008;

(b) "fee notice" means a notice of—

(i) the amount of a trial fee;

(ii) the trial fee payment date; and

(iii) the consequences of non-payment of the trial fee;

(c) "trial date" means the date of the trial in relation to which the trial fee is payable, and if the trial in relation to which the trial fee is payable is scheduled to commence during the course of a specified period, "trial date" means the date of the Monday of the first week of that specified period;

(d) "trial fee" means fee 2.1 set out in the Table in Schedule 1 to the Fees Order 20083 and payable for the trial of a case on the multi-track, fast track or small claims track;

(e) "trial fee payment date" means the date by which the trial fee must be paid, calculated in accordance with the Fees Order 2008;

(f) "revised trial fee payment date" means, if an application for fee remission is denied in whole or part, the revised date by which the fee or part of it is to be paid, calculated in accordance with the Fees Order 2008.

(2) This rule applies in relation to trial fees where that fee is to be paid by the claimant and the court notifies the parties in writing of the trial date.

(3) When the court notifies the parties in writing of the trial date, the court must also send a fee notice to the claimant.

(4) The fee notice may be contained in the same document as the notice of trial date, or may be a separate document.

(5) Where an application for full or part remission of a trial fee is refused, when the court sends written notice to the claimant of the refusal, the court must also notify the claimant in writing—

(a) that the claimant is required to pay the full trial fee by the revised trial fee payment date; and

(b) of the consequences of non-payment of the trial fee.

(6) Where part remission of a fee is granted, when the court sends written notice to the claimant of the part remission, the court must also notify the claimant in writing—

(a) that the claimant is required to pay the balance of the trial fee by the revised trial fee payment date; and

(b) of the consequences of non-payment of the balance of the trial fee.

(7) If—

(a) the claimant has had notice in accordance with this rule to pay the trial fee;

(b) the claimant has not applied to have the trial fee remitted in whole or part; and

(c) the trial fee has not been paid on or before the trial fee payment date,

the claim will automatically be struck out without further order of the court, and unless the court orders otherwise, the claimant will be liable for the costs which the defendant has incurred.

(8) If—

(a) the claimant has had notice in accordance with this rule to pay the trial fee;

(b) the claimant has applied to have the trial fee remitted in whole or part;

(c) remission is refused or only part remission of the trial fee is granted;

(d) following the decision on remission, the claimant has had notice in accordance with this rule to pay the full trial fee or balance of it; and

(e) the full trial fee or balance of it (as appropriate) has not been paid on or before the revised trial fee payment date,

the claim will automatically be struck out without further order of the court, and, unless the court orders otherwise, the claimant will be liable for the costs which the defendant has incurred.

So, CPR 3.7A1 imposes an obligation on a claimant to pay a trial fee.

1. When the court notifies the parties in writing of the trial date, the court must also send a fee notice to the claimant.

2. That notice must give a "trial fee payment date".

3. If the claimant does not make payment (or make an application for remission of fees) by the trial fee payment date then the action is automatically struck out.

The Trial Fee Payment Date

A lot of courts give notices of trial date well in advance of the trial date and the notices often give a trial fee payment date well in advance of the trial fee payment date.

However, the "trial fee payment" date is in fact set by the rules.

CPR 3,7A1 defines the trial fee payment date.

> *(e) "trial fee payment date" means the date by which the trial fee must be paid, calculated in accordance with the Fees Order 2008;*

The Fees Order 2008

Para. 2.1 in column 1 of the table at Sch. 1 to the Civil Proceedings Fees Order 2008 as amended ("the Fees Order 2008") sets the trial fee payable and provides:

> *'Where notice of trial date or trial period is given by the court 36 days or more before the trial date or the Monday of the first week of the notified trial period, fee 2.1 is payable at least 28 days prior to the trial date or the Monday of the first week of the notified trial period.'*

When less than 36 days' notice of the trial date is given, the Fees Order 2008 states that the trial fee is payable "within 7 days after the date on which such notice [of the trial date] is given".

Therefore:

- When the court gives 36 days (or more) notice of the trial date the trial fee must be made "at least 28 days prior to the trial date".

- If there is less than 36-days notice the fee must be paid within 7 days after the date of the date on which the notice must be given.

If a Court orders payment to be made more than 28 days before the trial, this is contrary to the Rules and it should be possible to argue that the striking out sanction should not apply under CPR 3.7A1). Even though payment is sent after the date stated in the fee notice, the rules do not give the court a discretion as to when the trial fee payment date should fall. When the trial is listed more than 36 days ahead of time, the trial fee payment date is set by the Civil Proceedings Fees Order 2008 (as amended) at 28 days before the first day of the trial. The court does not have the power to set some earlier date in a fee notice; it is failure to pay by the date calculated according to the Civil Proceedings Fees Order 2008 that triggers the strike out, not failure to pay by an earlier date specified in a fee notice. That said, it is not a risk that we would recommend taking.

The date by which the trial fee must be paid calculated in accordance with the Fees Order 2008 is "at least 28 days prior to the trial date", in a case where notice of trial date is given more than 36 days in advance. When less than 36 days' notice of the trial date is given, the Fees Order 2008 states that the trial fee is payable "within 7 days after the date on which such notice [of the trial date] is given".

Para. 2.1 of Sch. 1 to the Fees Order 2008, does not entitle the Court to set an earlier date for payment than 28 days. The words "at least 28 days prior to" mean "by no later than 28 days before". Similarly, the words "within 7 days after the date on which such notice is given" in the case of a trial listed less than 36 days in advance do not permit the court to set a trial fee payment date of a different number of days after the listing notice was given.

CPR 3.7A1(1)(b) requires a fee notice to be sent to the claimant which states the trial fee payment date. The trial fee payment date is not defined by CPR 3.7A1 as the date stated in the fee notice. It is defined as the date by which the trial fee must be paid calculated in accordance with the Fees Order 2008. So, if the date stated is not calculated in accordance with the Fees Order 2008, CPR 3.7A1(1)(e) and 3.7A1(7) have the effect that it is the date by which the trial fee must be paid in accordance with the Fees Order 2008 that triggers the sanction under CPR 3.7A1, not the date misstated in the fee notice.

A reason not to construe the Fees Order 2008 as permitting a court officer to set a date for payment of the hearing fee far in advance of the trial is that the Civil Proceedings Fees (Amendment) Order 2016, which introduced the automatic strike out provisions in their current form, also removed the claimant's right to repayment of the trial fee if the case should settle before trial (rather unfairly in my view). While there is a risk of the claimant paying a non-refundable trial fee for no benefit when the fee must be paid by 28 days before trial, that risk would significantly increase if the fee had to be paid many months before the trial according to a court officer's discretion. That is unlikely to have been the intention of Parliament. That said, the Court of Appeal has not yet ruled on the point and perhaps might consider that the Court can still impose a sanction given that an order has been made.

CHAPTER EIGHT
OTHER BREACHES OF THE RULES AND ORDERS

There is no limit to the number of situations where relief from sanction may be needed as it applies to the breach of any rule, order or Practice direction and is being adopted in other Tribunals than the Civil Courts. It even applies to implied sanctions that are not expressed in an order but which follow as a matter of logic. The only exception is extensions of time for Service of the Claim Form to which a separate Chapter is devoted.

The General Form of Judgment now includes the general catch all:

> "*Warning: you must comply with the terms imposed on you by this order: otherwise your case is liable to be struck out or some other sanction imposed. If you cannot comply you are expected to male a formal application to the Court before any deadline imposed upon you expires.*"

In case there was any doubt, this makes it crystal clear that the Court may impose sanctions whatever orders are breached.

In this chapter we look at recent situations where parties have applied for relief, to illustrate the current approach that the Court takes to such applications and the wide range of scenarios in which they can become necessary. There are other older cases concerning late service of witness statements and expert evidence, for example, which all trim on their own facts.

A table containing details of other cases on relief from sanction produced by St Johns Chambers can be found following this link: http://www.stjohnschambers.co.uk/dashboard/wp-content/uploads/Relief-from-Sanction.pdf

1. Issuing Proceedings

There is a separate chapter concerning serving the Claim Form, but other issues arise regarding issuing proceedings.

2. Group Litigation Orders

Kimathi v The Foreign & Commonwealth Office [2017] EWHC 939 (QB)

This case highlights the application of the *Denton* principles in the context of group litigation, where claimants have missed the cut-off date for adding their claims to the group register. It suggests that, where a Group Litigation Order (GLO) has been made to enable claims to be managed together so that costs are not disproportionate, the court may give even more weight than usual to the need to enforce compliance with rules, practice directions and orders.

Background

32 Claimants applied for an order granting relief from sanctions and permitting their claims to be added to the group register for the Kenyan Emergency Group Litigation, despite having failed to comply with the "cut-off date" in the GLO for claims to be added to the group register without permission of the court.

By the time of the application, the trial was well underway.

Decision

The court refused the application.

The judge said that to add a new type of claim nearly three years after the cut-off date would be wholly wrong in all the circumstances of the case, including because all solicitors involved in the litigation had abided by the decision that such claims would not be litigated, and there were no test claimants in this category.

In respect of the other applicants, there was some limited information which showed that there may be reasons these claims had not been entered onto the group register initially (ie because they did not suffer any injuries).

It was therefore not possible for the court to assume that the default in not registering the applicants was entirely that of the Solicitors rather than the applicants personally. In any event, in the judge's view, there was no good reason for the default, whether caused by the solicitors or the applicants.

The judge also took into account the fact that the application was far from prompt, as well as his conclusions that the breach was serious and significant and there was no good reason for it. In conclusion he said the application should not be granted, commenting that to do so would undermine the discipline of the litigation and render the cut-off date meaningless.

3. Permission to Issue Proceedings

Wilton UK Ltd & Anor v Shuttleworth & Ors [2018] EWHC 911 (Ch)

The judge was considered whether permission to continue derivative company proceedings should be given pursuant to s.263 Companies Act 2006 and whether retrospective permission should be granted to begin the proceedings, so validating certain steps that should have been taken only with permission of the court. The Denton issues related to the grant of retrospective permission.

The judge looked at the interrelationship between relief from sanction and CPR Rule 6.15(2). He ruled that:

"...the distinction drawn by Lord Sumption between cases involving relief from sanctions, itself encompassing weight being given to the factor of the disciplinary element of the CPR, and the provisions of CPR r6.15 is not one that, in my judgment, holds good for retrospective permission regarding the bringing of derivative proceedings and a factor which puts the exercise of the relevant discretion in that context on the CPR r6.15(2) side of the line.

True it is that I have held that the ability to grant retrospective permission and the effects of permission not having been granted are regulated by statute rather than the CPR. Nevertheless, in my view the process and timing of permission being regulated by the CPR (just as the process and timing of permission to appeal is regulated by the CPR though the requirement for permission is (largely) statutory see e.g. s54 Access to Justice Act 1999), the failure to obtain permission should be viewed as carrying a sanction (see, by analogy, the position regarding appeals).

Accordingly, I also reject the claimant's case (at least as I understood it at one point to be) that the matter is simply one at large to be considered against all the circumstances and that I should simply apply a "best interests of justice" test.

In reality, each of the three tests, that under CPR r6.15(2), that under Denton for relief from sanctions and that advocated by the claimant of "the best interests of justice" are directed at the court achieving a just result in all the circumstances. The circumstances in which the issue arises are capable of giving rise to a different structure of questions to determine what is just. In my judgment, each test involves application of a different structure to reach the "just" result in that each involves particular questions being asked in a structured process so as to assist in identifying the key considerations. Further, each results in different emphasis or weight being given to particular factors. Thus, to take one example, the disciplinary factor of encouraging rule compliance and effect on third parties carries less if any weight in carrying out the CPR r6.15(2) test compared with the Denton test."

The judge applied the relief from Sanctions test:

> *"In my assessment the breach was serious and significant. The making of an application for permission was simply not pursued and instead the proceedings were continued with. One point of the procedure is to weed out unmeritorious claims and to ensure that defendants (and companies) are not troubled by them. Although this has not turned out to be such a case, the breach of the rules (and the statute) was serious and/or significant.*
>
> *The reason given for not putting the matter before the court was essentially one that it would be better for the evidence to be in a better state than proceeding on inadequate evidence. In my view, this is not a satisfactory explanation. The matter should have been placed before the court well before expiry of the validity of the claim form so the court could judge whether the case should be got on with and make directions accordingly and/or whether there should be limited permission to serve documents or not. Instead of that the claimant took the matter out of the court's hands. Although I understand some of the reason for the delays in getting the case ready for the hearing that eventually took place I am not satisfied that they can be fully excused.*
>
> *Turning to, and in looking at, all the circumstances, I take into account that the breach in this case was not abusive in the sense of recklessness or a deliberate self-serving breach. The breach occurred in circumstances where the decision was an error as to what the overriding objective required rather than a deliberate abuse.*
>
> *I also take into account the fact that the defendants have not in reality been much harmed by the delay. At most an inter-parties application may have occurred a little earlier. The defendants were however properly served in terms of mode and time of service. Their complaint is one of lack of authority, which can now be rectified.*
>
> *I take into account the fact that all of the facts will have to be gone into on the Direct Claim and that the Derivative Claim of itself*

> *should not add too much to the overall costs (though I also bear in mind the difference in the identity of the parties in the two proceedings and particularly the defendants). It would be unjust if causes of action were made out in the Direct Claim but which were only vested in the company and which could not be pursued because I now refused relief."*

The judge signalled that such applications should not become routine.

> *"I am acutely aware of the need not to encourage (a) the subversion of the statutory process by bringing about rolled up applications such as this as routine (though in some cases it may well be sensible to agree the same) and (b) the need to avoid encouraging claimants bringing these claims to think that they can sit back and if the merits are otherwise on their side, rely on the court giving retrospective permission. However, I do take into account the point that, in light of this judgment, the appropriate approach will have been reinforced and claimants will have less excuse for taking such a course as was taken by the claimant in this case."*

4. Challenges To Jurisdiction

Apex Global Management v Global Torch [2017] EWCA Civ 315

This case suggests that, where a party may wish to challenge the court's jurisdiction in some circumstances, the point that should be raised early, even where the basis for challenge will only arise if the party's primary case is unsuccessful. Otherwise the court may find that the right to challenge jurisdiction has been lost due to the delay in making the application.

Background

In the underlying dispute, the parties each brought unfair prejudice petitions against one another. They relied on competing versions of a share sale and purchase agreement (SPA), each alleging that the other version was forged.

The court ultimately entered judgment in favour of the respondent on its counterclaim, having found that the version of the SPA relied on by the respondent was the true version. The petitioner then applied for a stay of execution of the judgment on the basis that the respondent's version of the SPA contained an exclusive jurisdiction clause in favour of the courts of Saudi Arabia. It argued that once the judge had reached that conclusion, he should have declined jurisdiction on the basis of the clause.

The judge refused the application for a stay of execution and the petitioner appealed.

Decision

The Court of Appeal dismissed the appeal on various bases, including on the basis of the petitioner's lateness in challenging jurisdiction.

Under CPR Part 11, a party who wishes to challenge the court's jurisdiction must make an application within 14 days after filing an acknowledgement of service. A party who fails to do so is deemed to have accepted that the English court has jurisdiction.

A late application for a stay was in substance an application for relief from sanctions and so had to be determined in accordance with the three-stage test established in Denton. In the court's judgment, the application of this test clearly resulted in a refusal of the application. The decisive factor was the lateness of the petitioner's jurisdiction challenge.

The court rejected the petitioner's argument that the proper time to make the application in relation to the jurisdiction clause was after the judge had handed down judgment; it was open to the petitioner to seek to reserve its position in relation to jurisdiction, even while disputing that the true contract contained any such jurisdiction clause.

The petitioner could not, in the court's view, remain silent about the effect of the jurisdiction clause until after judgment had been given on the basis of not extant issues relating to jurisdiction. The court added: "The obvious but fundamental point is that challenges to jurisdiction must be made as early as possible."

5. Security for Costs

Michael Wilson & Partners Limited v Sinclair and others

In this case, the claimant's claims for breach of contract and fiduciary duty had been struck out by the Commercial Court. Rix LJ granted permission to appeal against the strike out order. He ordered the claimant to pay certain sums in to the Court Funds Office by certain dates, including as security for costs of the appeal, failing which the appeal would be stayed. He refused to make an "unless order" that the appeal be dismissed unless the sums were paid, but he indicated that the claimant was "likely to find itself in grave difficulties" if it missed the deadlines and the appeal was stayed.

The claimant made the payments some 16 weeks late and then applied to lift the stay. The defendant applied to strike out the appeal.

At a hearing Lewison LJ refused the application to lift the stay, saying it was in effect an application for relief from sanction. He applied the Mitchell guidance, as he understood it at the time: it was not a trivial breach and there was no good reason for it; the paramount considerations were as stated in CPR 3.9 (the need to conduct litigation efficiently, and enforce compliance with rules and orders); and there was no conceivable ground on which the stay should be lifted. Therefore the appeal should be struck out.

Shortly after the Court of Appeal's judgment in Denton, the claimant applied to revoke Lewison LJ's order under CPR 3.1(7).

Decision

The Court of Appeal set aside the order and granted relief from sanction, thereby reinstating the appeal.

Applying Denton, although the breach was "significant or serious", and there was no good reason for it, applying the third stage of the Denton test meant relief should be granted. The problem with Lewison LJ's approach was that he went beyond attaching particular importance to the two CPR 3.9 factors, as Denton required; he treated them as paramount considerations which were effectively determinative against the grant of relief. He did not have regard to all the circumstances of the case, as Denton had stressed must be done.

Considering all the circumstances, it was appropriate to grant relief. The court noted in particular that Rix LJ had imposed only a stay, not a strike-out, as the consequence of missing the deadline, and that strike-out is a sanction of last resort. The court would therefore not have expected Lewison LJ to move straight from the stay to a strike-out unless there was a continuing default and a further opportunity, by way of a specific unless order, to remedy the default. Lewison LJ had given no separate consideration to whether a strike-out was a proportionate sanction.

It was appropriate to exercise the court's discretion under CPR 3.1(7) to revisit Lewison LJ's order. Although a change in the law, or the understanding of the law, would not generally provide a good reason for allowing earlier appellate decisions to be reopened, the circumstances of this case were exceptional. Mitchell, as the first decision of the Court of Appeal on the new wording of CPR 3.9, gave important guidance as to the proper approach in dealing with applications for relief from sanctions. But as the court made clear in Denton, that guidance, or the way it was widely understood, led to decisions that were manifestly unjust and disproportionate. It was also important that the application had been made promptly after the judgment in Denton was handed down.

Singh & Ors v The Charity Commission & Ors [2017] EWHC 2183 (Ch)

This case stemmed from the Claimant's failure to make a £75,000.00 payment on account of costs in accordance with an Unless Order. This resulted in the Claimant's claim being struck out and resulted in the Claimant being debarred from defending the counterclaim and having their Defence to the counterclaim struck out. The Claimants did make the payment 6 days late, however by this stage the claim had been struck out. The parties were in agreement that the breach was serious and the no good reason was provided for failing to comply with the Unless Order. Nevertheless, relief from sanctions was granted for three main reasons. First, because the payment was made shortly after the deadline within the Unless Order. Secondly because the court timetable would not be significantly affected (the dates for the pre-trial review and the trial itself still being available). Thirdly because the sanctions would affect other parties apart from the Claimants immediately before the court. As such 'standing back and looking at the overall justice of both side's cases, this is an appropriate case for relief from sanctions.'

It does seem to me that parties who are late in payment of security for costs stand a good chance of obtaining relief following these cases, but relief from sanctions adds an extra layer to the legal arguments.

6. Directions Questionnaires and Implied Sanctions

Solland International Limited v Clifford Harris & Co

The claimants issued proceedings against the defendant for alleged negligence in the conduct of earlier High Court litigation.

Allocation questionnaires were due to be filed by a certain date. The defendant filed its questionnaire on that date, but the claimants did not lodge their questionnaire or take any further step in the action, other than lodging a notice of change of solicitors, until after the defendant applied to strike out the claim. The claimants then filed their allocation questionnaire and retrospective application for an extension of time and, as necessary, relief from sanction.

This is something that quite often happens where a party fails to file its Directions Questionnaire and the Court may issue an Unless order or strike out the defaulting party's case as nothing causes more delay, perhaps, as the Court cannot issue any directions in the case to progress it.

Decision

The judge struck out the claim as an abuse of process.

He first considered whether the delay of 31 months in filing the allocation questionnaire gave rise to a sanction in respect of which relief must be sought and granted before the claimants could continue their claim. He concluded that it did not. The only sanction for failure to file an allocation questionnaire was that the court would give any direction it considered appropriate; here no direction had been made as a result of the breach.

The Master said that where, as here, there was an express sanction provided by the rules, albeit that it was in the discretion of the court, there could be no room for an implied sanction. Further, it was not a default which, absent an appropriate extension, had the effect of precluding a claim being advanced so that an implicit sanction arose. This was in contrast to, for example, a notice of appeal.

Another example the Master gave was a failure to file a defence in time which, he said, would mean that the defence simply could not be pursued unless an extension was given. Arguably, however, there is an express sanction for failure to file a defence in time, which is to leave open the possibility of judgment in default being entered; if default judgment is not filed, it is not clear that relief is needed. Entering judgment in default amounts to a sanction for the purposes of CPR 3.9, and an application to set aside default judgment should be treated as an application for relief from sanction.

In this case, however, although the Master held there was no need to obtain relief from sanction, it was appropriate to strike out the claim as an abuse of process. This was principally on the ground that the claimants had pursued the litigation without any settled intention to progress the claim to a trial or other proper conclusion, in knowing disregard of the rules and their obligation to pursue the claim diligently.

It would appear that this decision is rather unreliable as most practitioners would consider the failure to file direction questionnaires on time to be a breach which requires relief and there is often an express sanction now for failure to file on time in any event.

7. Unless orders

By their very nature "unless" orders are meant to be the end of the line, so it should be no surprise if relief from sanctions is difficult to obtain where an unless order has been flouted.

Micheal -v- Phillips [2017] EWHC 42 (QB)

This case relates to inadequate disclosure; retention of electronic documents and peremptory orders. Things did not go well for the party in default.

The Defendant failed to provide proper disclosure as required by directions, so the Claimant applied for an Unless Order that they do so. The Defendant agreed to the making of the Unless Order. The Defendant proceeded to disclose documents electronically, just an hour before the deadline indicated within the Unless Order. Hard copies were sent thereafter. On review the disclosure was deemed to be inadequate by the Claimant and the Claimant applied to have the Defence and Counterclaim stuck out accordance with the Unless Order. The Defendant provided extensive reasons as to why the disclosure did not take place in accordance with the Unless Order, most notably a cyber-attack on their computer systems. Upon investigation the judge was not persuaded by these reasons. With the insufficient disclosure unfairly prejudicing the

Claimant's ability to prepare for trial and with the Defendant having agreed to the terms of the Consent Order, no relief was awarded.

The Defendant's explanations for their failure to provide disclosure or preserve their computer hardware were unsatisfactory for a variety of reasons.

- The Defendant had entered into the unless order by consent and had thereby voluntarily accepted the proportionality of the sanction for non- compliance. They could not now argue it was disproportionate.
- The profoundly unsatisfactory way in which the electronic data had been lost or suppressed was also relevant.
- The Court was not able to assess the relative merits of the respective arguments in order to factor that into the weighing exercise in the third stage.

The Court found that:

> *"Given the scale of the non-observance of the Order it is unnecessary to dwell in detail upon other matters. However there are a number of additional points to make. First, the failures significantly and unfairly prejudice the ability of the Claimants to prepare for trial. This is a case which will turn upon the forensic analysis of underlying financial data. A great deal of the most important documentation and data has been withheld from the Claimants by the Defendants. Second, the Defendants entered into the Unless Order by consent. The proportionality of the sanction for non-compliance was thus voluntarily accepted by them. It is of little moment to complain now that to visit the consented to sanction upon the Defendants is disproportionate. Third, I take into account the history of this case and the profoundly unsatisfactory way in which electronic data has been suppressed and/or lost"*

It was agreed that the defendants' breaches were serious and there was no good reason. The. Court made the following comments:

> *"**I turn now to consider the real dispute between the parties which is whether it is just in all the circumstances to grant the Defendants' application for relief from sanctions. For all the reasons that I set out below I have come to the conclusion that: there remains serious outstanding breaches of the Unless Order; that I should refuse the application for relief; and, that I should therefore grant the Claimants' application for an order that the Defence and Counterclaim of the First and Second Defendants be struck out and that they be debarred from defending the claim.***
>
> *I start by considering whether, as of today, in the period shortly prior to trial, the First and Second Defendants have complied with their disclosure obligations pursuant to the Unless Order. **As to this I am satisfied that even now there is a substantial failure to comply with the Unless Order.** There are many instances of breach. I do not propose to examine every particular instance of non-compliance. Instead I propose to focus upon the principal failings that have been identified in the present case. I also consider below other factors potentially relevant to the analysis."*
>
> *"**I am wholly unsatisfied by the explanations given by the Defendants to account for the failure, on their part, to provide disclosure and/or to preserve the hardware.**"*

<u>Schenk v Cook [2017] EWHC 144 (QB)</u>

In this matter, a Defendant breached an Unless Order regarding disclosure and had their Defence struck out. The failings were determined to be serious in that they represented the culmination of a series of defaults on the part of the Defendant. The Defendant's conduct prior to the breach was taken into account when considering the seriousness of the breach itself. The Defendant was found to have no good reason for the breach and based on these factors the judge did not grant Relief.

Failings leading to the strike out of the defence had been serious. They represented the culmination of a series of repeat defaults that had justified the unless order. The defaults were not trivial but related to potentially central matters in dispute.

It was appropriate to have regard to the overall merits of the case. The merits would normally, but not inevitably, be irrelevant. The extent to which they could be taken into account in a given case was fact sensitive. Given the way the instant trial had come to be conducted, it had been possible to conclude that the merits lay with the Claimant against the Defendant. However, because of the way the trial had unfolded, the merits of the instant case were not a precedent for other cases on that point.

This case serves as a reminder that the Court will take into account the history of the case and whether there have been other breaches of orders along the way. The Court will also have regard to the overall merits of the case.

Falmouth House Ltd v Micha'al Kamel Abou-Hamdan [2017] EWHC 779 (Ch)

This case concerned the breach of an unless order. The Defence struck out. The Order had required appellant to attend trial in person. They did not attend and Counsel attended on their behalf.

The breach was not serious or significant as it would have made no difference to the respondent, the court, the conduct of the litigation or the conduct of any other litigation whether the appellant was physically present during the trial. The Court had look at the purpose of the order which was to ensure the trial went ahead.

Looking at the purpose of the order is sensible in the circumstances in order to avoid a draconian outcome. Sometimes the Court will order a party to attend for cross examination and in those circumstances it is hard to justify relief from sanction.

The Financial Conduct Authority v Da Vinci Invest Ltd & Ors` [2017] EWHC 2220 (Ch)

This is a case involving a litigant in person and breach of an unless order. In The Financial Conduct Authority v Da Vinci Invest Ltd & Mr Justice Snowden rejected a defendant's application for relief from sanctions for breach of an unless order. The application involved a contention that a defendant was unaware that solicitors had been acting on his behalf and knew nothing about the action.

The claimant brought proceedings against several defendants. The defendant, Mr Pornye, had solicitors who said they were acting on his behalf, they solicitors came off record, and judgment was entered after a trial at which he did not attend.

Subsequently Mr Pornye applied to set aside the judgment. He alleged that the solicitors who had represented him did so without authority and he had no knowledge of the matter. During the course of the application the judge made unless orders that he provide documents in support of the application. He did not comply with the order. After time for compliance was past he applied to vary it.

In respect of the first stage of the test, the seriousness and significance of the breach, it had been alleged that the Defendant did not have any, or any formal notice of the proceedings against him; and that his signature had been forged on the Defence and witness statement by someone else. The failure by Mr. Pornye to comply fully with the February Order, which followed a hearing at which he had been present and which he plainly understood, and the Unless Order which had been translated into Hungarian for him, meant that his own Set Aside Application could not progress.

The Court reiterated the position regarding unless orders. As Jackson LJ indicated in British Gas Trading v Oak Cash and Carry [2016] 1 WLR 4530 at paragraph 41,

> *"The very fact that X has failed to comply with an "unless" order (as opposed to an "ordinary" order) is undoubtedly a pointer towards seriousness and significance. This is for two reasons. First, X is in breach of two successive obligations to do the same thing. Secondly, the court has underlined the importance of doing that thing by specifying an automatic sanction in default (in this case the draconian sanction of strike out)."*

Although Jackson LJ went on (at paragraph 42) to accept that not every breach of an "unless" order is serious and significant (giving as an example the filing of a costs budget 45 minute late), the instant case is not such a case. Mr. Pornye had still not complied with the requirements of the Unless Order by the time of the hearing in October 2016.

As to the second stage, being the reasons for the breach, the Defendant argued that he needed, and was entitled by Article 6 of the European Convention on Human Rights to, a translation of all of the trial documents into Hungarian. However, neither Mr. Pornye's application nor his submissions specifically explained why he failed to comply with the February order or the Unless Order.

The judge said that "The only other substantive point made by Mr. Pornye was that he had been working in a holiday resort outside Budapest over the summer months and had not been able to attend to the case. I do not think that this excuses Mr. Pornye's failure to comply with orders that should have been attended to before the summer started. The requirements of the orders were not onerous and were essential to enable the Set Aside Application to be progressed efficiently."

Regarding the third stage, dealing justly with the application the Judge emphasised that

> *"34. Factor (a) [in CPR 3.9(1)] makes it clear that the court must consider the effect of the breach in every case. If the breach has prevented the court or the parties from conducting the litigation (or other litigation) efficiently and at proportionate cost, that will be a*

factor weighing in favour of refusing relief. Factor (b) emphasises the importance of complying with rules, practice directions and orders. This aspect received insufficient attention in the past. The court must always bear in mind the need for compliance with rules, practice directions and orders, because the old lax culture of non-compliance is no longer tolerated.

35. Thus, the court must, in considering all the circumstances of the case so as to enable it to deal with the application justly, give particular weight to these two important factors. In doing so, it will take account of the seriousness and significance of the breach (which has been assessed at the first stage) and any explanation (which has been considered at the second stage). The more serious or significant the breach the less likely it is that relief will be granted unless there is a good reason for it. Where there is a good reason for a serious or significant breach, relief is likely to be granted. Where the breach is not serious or significant, relief is also likely to be granted.

36. But it is always necessary to have regard to all the circumstances of the case. The factors that are relevant will vary from case to case. As has been pointed out in some of the authorities that have followed the Mitchell case [2014] 1 WLR 795, the promptness of the application will be a relevant circumstance to be weighed in the balance along with all the circumstances. Likewise, other past or current breaches of the rules, practice directions and court orders by the parties may also be taken into account as a relevant circumstance.

....

44. We should also make clear that the culture of compliance that the new rules are intended to promote requires that judges ensure that the directions that they give are realistic and achievable. It is no use imposing a tight timetable that can be seen at the outset to be unattainable. The court must have regard to the realities of litigation in making orders in the first place. Judges should also have in mind, when making directions, where the Rules provide for automatic sanctions in the case of default. Likewise, the parties should be aware of these consequences when they are agreeing directions. "Unless" orders should be reserved for situations in which they are truly required: these are usually so as to enable the litigation to proceed efficiently and at proportionate cost."

The judge considered that the Defendant's failure to comply with the order from February and the Unless Order has prevented the Set Aside Application from being proceeded with efficiently, or at proportionate cost. The Defendant has also failed to comply with other orders and directions from the court.

The Judge also found that the underlying merits of the set aside application was not strong and for all those reasons the Court refused the application.

Even though the Defendant was a litigant in person, the Court adopted a tough line, looking at the underlying merits of the case.

8. Notice to Prove

Tuke v JD Classics Ltd [2018] EWHC 531 (QB)

This case concerned a "Notice to Prove" the authenticity of documents. The claimant brought an action claiming an account and and delivery up of all documents relating to the defendant's sale of classic cars on his behalf. His case was that the defendant had not properly accounted for the sums the cars were sold for. The defendant made an application for summary judgment, that was not successful. One of the issues the judge had to consider was the claimant's service of a Notice to Prove. The claimant's case was that some of the documents produced by the defendant were not authentic.

Mr Justice Julian Knowles granted a claimant relief from sanctions. The judge considered that:

> *"It would in my judgment be artificial and not in accordance with the overriding requirement to deal with cases justly and at proportionate cost to allow this case to go forward on the basis of a deemed acceptance of genuineness of the invoices when the factual reality is different and has been known at all times by both sides to be different and the matter has been squarely put in issue in the proceedings and has been dealt with in evidence by Mr Hood on behalf of the Defendant"*

The Notice to Prove, dated 6 February 2018, was served on 7 February 2018. It required the Defendant to prove certain invoices, namely (a) those invoices said to have been issued to Mr Tuke but not received by him at the time, and (b) those invoices purportedly issued to third parties, but which have been disclosed only in redacted form.

The Defendant's solicitors responded to that Notice to Prove on 7 February 2018, claiming that it was served out of time as it should have been served by 24 August 2017, which was the date by which witness statements had to be served.

The judge agreed agree that the Notice to Admit was not served in time in accordance with CPR r 32.19, He went on to say:

> *"I must first consider the seriousness and significance of the Claimant's failure to give the required notice. In my judgment, it was neither serious nor significant, on the facts of this case. The Defendant was not misled in any way by the Claimant's failure. I accept that the Defendant has known since at least August 2017 that the Claimant was doubting the authenticity of these documents. The Defendant cannot properly have genuinely believed that there had been a considered change of position by the Claimant on this issue, which is why no doubt Mr Hood dealt with the matter in his witness statement, as I have explained.*
>
> *I must then consider why the default occurred. As I have said, it occurred through the oversight of Mr Tuke's legal team. Mr Brannigan candidly accepted there was no real excuse for the failure.*

Thirdly, I have to consider all the circumstances of the case, giving particular weight (in accordance with the guidance given in Denton) to the need for litigation to be conducted efficiently and at proportionate cost and to enforce compliance with rules, practice directions and orders, in the language of CPR r 3.9. As to this, there is of course a requirement on litigants and their lawyers to comply with the CPR, and I give this very serious weight. 'Rules are rules', as Mr Pymont put it. But this is not a case of a deliberate and intentional flouting of a rule designed to deliberately wrong foot an opponent. This was an honest oversight by those advising Mr Tuke, and no doubt the point has been taken on board for the future. It would in my judgment be artificial and not in accordance with the overriding requirement to deal with cases justly and at proportionate cost to allow this case to go forward on the basis of a deemed acceptance of genuineness of the invoices when the factual reality is different and has been known at all times by both sides to be different and the matter has been squarely put in issue in the proceedings and has been dealt with in evidence by Mr Hood on behalf of the Defendant.

Taking these matters together, in my judgment it is in the interests of justice to extend time for the service of the Notice to Prove and to grant relief from sanctions."

Given the other authorities, the judge was perhaps generous in this decision but it illustrates that the Courts are much more willing to allow relief following Denton.

9. Extension of Stays

Regarding extending stays, the order will often say that:

"*On or before x date one of the following steps must be taken*

Either

> *The Claimant must notify the Court that the whole of the claim has settled*
>
> *Or*
>
> *The Claimant or defendant must write to the court requesting an extension of the stay period, explaining the steps being taken towards settlement and identifying any mediator expert or other person helping with the process*
>
> *The letter should confirm the agreement of all the other parties*
>
> *Or*
>
> *All the parties must file a completed directions questionnaire at the Court. Where a settlement of some of the issues in dispute has been reached a list of those issues should be attached to the completed questionnaire. The list must be agreed with the other parties and must indicate that it has been agreed."*

The order then goes on to say that "under CPR 3.1a) the Court will generally accept a letter from any party, or from the solicitor for any party, as an application to extend the stay under rule 26.4. The letter in this instance should be treated as an application or indication of any application and therefore the relevant fee should be charged as per the Fee order. The current charge is £100."

With some stay orders, the Court orders that the parties write to the Court or make an application for an extension of the stay before x date failing which the claim will be struck out without further order. Solicitors often forget to do this and are then left having to make an application for relief.

10. Adjourning Trials

<u>Dove v London Borough of Havering [2018] EWCA Civ 156</u>

Perhaps the cases which the Court takes most seriously are those involving the loss of a trial date.

In Dove -v- London Borough of Havering the Court of Appeal considered a number of procedural issues prior to giving judgment. The defendants argued that they should have been granted an adjournment of the trial. The judge rejected that application. The judge's decision was upheld by the Court of Appeal. The Courts are generally reluctant to adjourn trials as it impacts upon the Courts' resources as well as affecting the other party.

The appellants appealed against an order giving possession on the ground of rent arrears. The judge had declined to grant an adjournment to the defendant tenants when legal aid had not been extended. The judge also refused an application on the grounds of ill-health and continued with the hearing on the third day when one of the defendants did not appear. The tenants took a number of procedural issues on the appeal.

The Court of Appeal found that:

> The judge "***did not approach the application as if it were an application for relief against sanctions. If he had done so he would have applied the well-known three stage test in Denton v TH White Ltd [2014] EWCA Civ 906, [2014] 1 WLR 3296. Rather, in my judgment he was referring to the serious consequences, discussed in Denton, of adjourning trials at the last moment.***

In Denton ... the court stressed the importance of ensuring that "hearings, once fixed, are not adjourned." In Denton itself the grant of relief against sanctions had necessitated the adjournment of the trial.

This court held that the judge had been plainly wrong. In their joint judgment Lord Dyson MR and Vos LJ said:

> *"An adjournment would result in the protraction of proceedings which had already dragged on for far too long. It would cause a waste of court resources and generate substantial extra costs for the parties. It would cause inconvenience to a large number of busy people, who had carved out space in their diaries for the anticipated trial."*

Jackson LJ said:

> *"The judge's order that the claimants pay "the defendant's costs thrown away by the vacation of the trial" does not begin to meet the justice of the case. There are many hidden costs flowing from adjournment of the trial: witness statements and reports need updating; fee earners handling the litigation may change with a need for newcomers to read into the case; both legal teams continue to work upon the litigation and so forth. In addition to the increased costs there is wastage of resources. Lawyers, experts, factual witnesses and other busy people who had cleared their diaries to attend the trial (probably cancelling other commitments) will have to clear their diaries yet again for another trial a year later. There is also the continuing strain on the parties to consider. What litigants need is finality, not procrastination. Quite apart from its impact on the immediate parties in Denton, the judge's order has caused unnecessary delay for many other litigants awaiting their day in court."*
>
> ***These considerations apply whatever the reason for the adjournment. There is no doubt that modern case management places considerable importance on not losing trial dates once they have been fixed.*** This is also reflected, for example, in PD 29 para 7.4 (1) which says:
>
> *"The court will not allow a failure to comply with directions to lead to the postponement of the trial unless the circumstances are exceptional."*

> *"Accordingly I do not consider that it can be said that the judge was wrong in his approach to a last minute application to adjourn the trial. In addition to the general undesirability of adjourning a trial to which all three members of the court adverted in Denton, there are, in my judgment, a number of factors specific to this case that militated against an adjournment. First the application was made very late. Second, the cause of the difficulty was Ms Dove's legal representatives' tardiness in applying for an extension of legal aid. Third, the trial date had already been adjourned once before. Fourth, rent at the full rate had not been paid for many years*. This was not simply a case of disruption to Havering: the debt was increasing week by week. There was no realistic prospect that the Misses Dove could pay off the arrears or even pay the current rent. *Fifth, there was no realistic prospect that the Misses Dove could pay the costs thrown away by an adjournment: and indeed there is no record of any offer by them to do so. Sixth, an adjournment would have caused disruption and inconvenience to other court users. Seventh, there was no certainty that an adjournment would serve any useful purpose*. Set against that was the difficulty, which the judge recognised, that the Misses Dove would face in defending the case without legal representation. *What weight to give each of these factors was essentially a matter for the judge. This court should not interfere with case-management decisions of this kind unless compelled to do so. I would reject this ground of appeal."*

In respect of ill health, the Court commented that:

> *"Where an application for an adjournment is made on medical grounds the court will normally expect to see evidence from a medical practitioner familiar with the patient and his or her medical condition. That evidence should identify what the medical condition is, and what features of it prevent participation in the trial process. The evidence should also provide a reasoned prognosis and describe what arrangements short of an adjournment could be made to accommodate a party's difficulties. Even then, the ultimate decision is for the court to make."*

It is clear that the Courts will be very reluctant to grant relief from sanction in relation to the adjournment of a trial unless there are exceptional circumstances and in the case of ill health, evidence put before the Court.

11. Appeals

R (On the Application of Kaur) v The Secretary of State Home Department [2017] EWCA Civ 821

The rules on relief from sanctions apply equally on appeals. This case illustrates the importance of making Applications as soon as it becomes apparent there will be a breach, even if the breach is outside of the Parties' control. The Appellant was required to file their Appeal and documents in support of the same. The Appeal itself was lodged correctly but the transcript which was required to be considered was not lodged in accordance with the rules. It emerged that this was because they had been unable to obtain the transcript. As a result of the failure to file the transcript, the Appeal was dismissed. The Appellant sought a review which was ultimately treated as an Application for relief from sanctions. It was established that the breach was serious but also that there was good reason for the failure to serve the transcript. Ultimately the Appellant should have applied in advance of the breach, knowing it would occur. Their failure to do so meant considering the matter generally there should be no relief.

Pinisetty -v-Manikonda [2017] EWHC 838 (QB)

This is a case where an appeal was lodged using the incorrect address. The Respondent lodged a Respondent's notice and cross-appeal by means of tracked DX. This was within the time limit required under the CPR. However, the covering letter was addressed to the "Appeals Office, Chancery Division" instead of the "Appeals Office Queens Bench Division". This documents had been lodged with the court within the prescribed time.

The court office neither forwarded the documents to the Queens Bench Division, nor returned them at the time, such that a replacement had to be filed.

The judge found that relief should be granted on the following basis:

> *"Applying that guidance, in my view the failure is neither serious nor significant. I have had a full explanation of why the default occurred and, to my mind of particular relevance to the third stage, the default is in itself very low on any scale of culpability. The deadline was well in mind. Steps were taken to meet it. Those steps would have been effective but for what might be thought to be a misdirection of the form to the particular division of the court, albeit it was the court which in another division was entitled to receive the form."*

> *"With very considerable hesitation, in this case I would have granted relief from sanction. I would have extended time. I would have done so because permission to appeal had already been given (by the lower court). The vice to which Mr Sawtell referred – that of the parties not knowing if their rights were or were not in jeopardy from an appeal - does not arise, unless the length of time taken in context within which the appeal was lodged was significant or substantial. It is part of setting the context for that, in dealing with the first question I am required to address by Denton, that I think that the fact permission to appeal had already been granted was relevant. If so, it was desirable generally that any cross-reference in a notice of appeal, albeit that it should be in rare cases only where that is required, was to the perfected judgment. Though I have regard to the circumstances amongst which is that the Claimant was in a position to proceed on 7th September and did not do so, the appeal file would only be progressed in the appeal court once a perfected judgment was received at the court office. Given the clear message from the email traffic that the appeal was to be pursued, I have come to the conclusion that the delay was neither serious nor significant taken in context."*

> *"I would not have found there to be any good reason for delay. It was never suggested by the Claimant herself that she was waiting for the*

> *perfected judgment, and that simply does not in any event stand with the chronology. The points Mr Sawtell makes are good ones, but cannot in the event answer the fact that not to extend time in these circumstances would be to rely heavily upon a formalism which had no meaningful or practical effect on either party or the progress of the appeal."*

The Court was persuaded that it would not be right to rely upon a formalism which had no meaningful effect. In other words, the Court looked at the prejudice suffered by the other party and they did not appear to be prejudiced. It was a case where the Respondent was relying on a technicality to deliver a knockout blow and following Denton the Courts are less likely to allow this.

<u>Patterson v Spencer [2017] EWCA Civ 140</u>

In Patterson -v- Spencer the Court granted relief from sanctions in a case where the judge had applied the Mitchell principles, pre Denton and it is perhaps unsurprising that the decision was moderated. The judge commented that:

> *"Lacking clairvoyance, the judge was understandably unable to forecast the revised guidance which this court would give in <u>Denton</u>, one month after the hearing before him."*

This was a situation where the failure by an appellant to file a transcript in accordance with a court order was a serious and significant breach.

The Court found that there was a good reason for the breach in that the appellant had not received the order. Therefore, in all the circumstances of this case it was appropriate to grant relief from sanctions.

> *"**The first question is whether the breach, viewed in isolation, was serious or significant**. Mr Macleod-James sought to persuade us that it was not. Viewed in context, it caused no more than a four week delay to an application for permission to appeal, and an extension of time for appealing, which was still at an early stage:*

*…**The failure to lodge a transcript of the judgment under appeal, within the period directed by the court, cannot be characterised as unserious or insignificant, because the application for permission to appeal could not be determined until the transcript was provided.** Of all the documents needed for the appeal, it was probably the most important…*

The next question is why the default occurred. As to this, I respectfully think the judge was wrong to disbelieve the explanation given by the Appellant, and he was unduly influenced by the absence of a separate witness statement from her.** It was entirely appropriate for her to give the evidence upon which she wished to rely in Part C of the application notice, and **in the absence of any evidence in answer from the Trustee she did not need to elaborate the explanation which she had given, even if she would have been well advised to do so (for example, by procuring a supporting statement from her neighbour, and/or by exhibiting to a statement the documents which she apparently provided at the hearing).

***If the Appellant's evidence was accepted at face value, she clearly had a good reason for failing to comply with the Unless Order before 21 March 2014, because she knew nothing about it.** It is true that she remained in breach of Arnold J's earlier order of 9 January, but as a litigant in person she may not have appreciated the importance of the distinction between the transcript of the proceedings, which she had supplied, and the judgment, which she had not. Furthermore, we do not know when the transcript of the judgment was sent to District Judge Clarke for approval, or when it was returned. The Appellant could no doubt have supplied this information had the deficiency in the bundle which she lodged been drawn to her attention; but there is no evidence that it was, and until she finally received the Unless Order, there was nothing to alert her to the problem.*

It is relevant to note, in this connection, that the Unless Order was made by Arnold J of his own initiative, without any applic-

ation having been made by the Trustee. *The papers were presumably referred back to him by the court staff, when they noted that the bundle lodged by the Appellant did not include a transcript of the judgment.* ***Thus the Appellant had no way of knowing that a further, more stringent, order was likely to be made against her,*** *and it is perfectly credible that the first she knew of the Unless Order was on 19 April 2014, nearly one month after the deadline for compliance with it had expired.*

In all the circumstances, I would conclude that the Appellant had a good reason for her failure to comply with the Unless Order.

As to the third <u>Denton</u> stage, it is appropriate to begin with the court's statement at [35] that "[w]here there is a good reason for a serious or significant breach, relief is likely to be granted". In the present case, that conclusion is reinforced by the fact that the appeal proceedings were still in their infancy, and no prejudice can have been caused to the Trustee apart from the relatively short delay in filing the transcript of the judgment. *As to the alleged earlier defaults by the Appellant, of which District Judge Clarke had taken such a dim view, it is worthy of note that the only order with which the Appellant had failed to comply was the July 2013 Order, and even then she might have had a respectable argument that she was not in breach of the timetable steps in paragraph (2) of that order, given the rather curious way in which it was framed, and that her only breach had been of the requirement in paragraph (3) to ensure that the timetable was met, and to notify the court promptly if it was not. Given the very serious ill health from which she suffered at the time, and in particular from September 2013 onwards, this breach was in my view at the lower end of the scale of seriousness, quite apart from the question whether it was ever appropriate to order the Appellant to ensure compliance with a timetable relating to the capacity of her father.*

In any event, ***despite the impression given by the District Judge's judgment, Mr Groves very properly accepted before us that the Appellant had not been guilty of repeated breaches of court orders.***

> *The exasperation which District Judge Clarke clearly felt seems rather to have been the product of what she perceived to be a series of delaying tactics for which the Appellant was one of the persons responsible. There may well have been some truth in this perception, but whether it justified the draconian step of barring the Appellant from defending the Trustee's underlying application is another matter. I do not share the judge's confidence that the Appellant's grounds of appeal are "not … at all persuasive", and I certainly do not consider that her appeal is so obviously hopeless on the merits that, for that reason alone, it should not be allowed to proceed to consideration of the application for permission to appeal by a Chancery judge in the usual way.*
>
> *All in all, I am satisfied that a consideration of all the circumstances of the case, and of the need to deal justly with the application for relief from sanctions, leads to the conclusion that relief should be granted. If McFarlane LJ agrees, that is therefore the order which I would make."*

The Court here allowed the litigant in person some leeway because she did not receive the unless order and may not have understood the difference between a transcript and a judgement. Moreover, the Court took into account the fact that the Unless order was a unilateral order of the Court's own motion and there had been no other breaches of orders. So this is an example of a softer approach where the Court might not have been so sympathetic if the appellant had not been a litigant in person.

Motley & Ors v Shadwell Park Ltd (2017) Ca (Civ Div) (Sharp LJ, Henderson Lj) 09/11/2017

A judge had erred in granting a party relief from sanctions under CPR r.3.9 and reinstating its appeal against the refusal of relief from forfeiture of a commercial lease which was struck out following its failure to comply with an unless order requiring it to lodge bundles and a skeleton by a certain date, following which the listed half-day appeal hearing in the High Court was lost. The respondent applied for relief from sanctions under CPR r.3.9. The judge found that the respondent's breach was serious because of the length of its delay and the loss of the appeal hearing date, and that there was no good reason for the default. He considered that a factor against the grant of relief was that the appellants would be prejudiced by being unable to re-let the land pending a relisted appeal, and that if the respondent won the appeal, they would not be able to recover rent for the intervening period. Against that background, he held that the loss of an appeal date might not be as significant as losing a trial date, and that it was right and just to grant relief because the respondent would otherwise lose a long lease, with its development potential, which was of greater significance than the potential prejudice to the appellants.

The appellants contended that, given the serious and significant breaches of court orders for which there was no good reason, there was no significant relevant factor on which the judge had been entitled to rely in granting relief from sanction, and that his decision had exceeded the wide ambit of his discretion under r.3.9.

The Court found that in circumstances where there had been a serious breach for no reason and an appeal hearing date had been lost, very significant factors were required to tip the scales in favour of granting relief. None of the factors the judge had identified fell into that category. Whilst the loss of a half-day appeal hearing might not be as serious as losing a trial date, it was still a factor weighing against the grant of relief. The loss of a half-day appeal in the High Court was serious because it impacted on other court users. The judge had failed to have regard to the appellants' reasonable expectation that the case would be dealt with efficiently and at proportionate cost, which it would not be if the appeal was relisted. Moreover, the judge had been wrong to have found that the prejudice to the respondent outweighed that caused to the appellants. The evidence of potential loss to the respondent was, at best, vague. On the true analysis, the loss to the respondent was derived from the general law of forfeiture and its obligation under the Tomlin order: the business opportunity relied on had already been lost, and its only loss was that of the opportunity to argue that the court below had been wrong. That situation arose whenever any case was struck out for non-compliance. There was nothing of substance to outweigh the first and second points in Denton. The judge's decision was set aside and the respondent's appeal therefore remained struck out.

12. Honesty

Wadsley v Sherwood Forest Hospitals NHS Foundation Trust

In this case there was doubt whether an employee of the Defendant's solicitors had told lies about whether a court order relating to service of witness statements had been complied with. The Defendants' solicitor said that statements had been served. The 9-day delay in serving statements had no impact on the litigation. Relief was granted after considering stages 2 and 3 as breach had been made more serious by the lies told. The Respondents has been right not to consent to the relief being granted. This case demonstrates that covering up a breach does not assist the applicant.

Clearly, where relief from sanctions is concerned, honesty is the best policy.

13. Overarching Principle – Don't Take Advantage

Viridor Waste Management v Veolia Environmental Services

The claimants issued a claim, claiming unjust enrichment in respect of payments made in excess of what had been due to the defendant, as a result of a Court of Appeal decision in relation to tax issues nearly six years earlier. Shortly afterwards, the defendant issued a separate claim against the claimant on similar grounds.

Under the terms of a consent order, the particulars of claim had to be filed and served by 14 January 2015. They were filed with the court on 12 January, but in error were posted by second-class post on 13

January, arriving at the defendant's solicitors offices on 15 January. There was some dispute as to whether this meant service was effected on 15 January, or at the latest 19 January (further service copies having been sent by various methods once the error was discovered).

The claimant applied for a retrospective extension of time for service, the defendant having refused to consent to an extension. The defendant applied to strike out the claim.

It was common ground that the application was for relief from sanctions under CPR 3.9 and that the Mitchell and Denton guidance applied.

Decision

The court (Popplewell J) granted relief from sanctions and awarded indemnity costs against the defendant.

Regardless of the precise date on which service was effected, what mattered in considering whether the breach was serious or significant was that the particulars had been received by the defendant's solicitors by lunchtime on 15 January. This was only a few working hours after the deadline. The delay had no real impact on the course of the litigation, the court, or other court users. It had not disrupted the process, save as a result of the application for relief and the resistance to that application. It was not a serious or significant breach.

The court rejected the defendant's argument that the delay was significant because of the limitation position, and that an extension would be tantamount to extending the limitation period. The court noted that it is the issue of the claim form that stops time running for limitation purposes. Service of particulars is, it said, a subsequent step in the proceedings which does not validate or invalidate the effect of issue of the claim form for limitation purposes.

Although it was not necessary to consider the other stages of the Denton test, the court considered them briefly for the sake of completeness. Although there was no good reason for the default, it was an accidental administrative error which was at the lower end of the scale of culpability. In considering all the circumstances of the case, the most significant factor was that if no extension was granted the claimant would be at risk of losing the benefit of a claim worth £27 million in circumstances where the defendant would be able to advance its mirror claim for around £32 million (unless the claimant was able to advance its claim as a counterclaim in the separate proceedings, though it was arguable that this would be an abuse of process). If the judge had concluded that the breach was serious or significant, he would have concluded the justice of the case required an extension to be granted.

The court also referred to the Court of Appeal's comments in Denton that it is wholly inappropriate for litigants to take advantage of mistakes by opposing parties in the hope that relief from sanctions would be denied and they would obtain a windfall strike-out or other litigation advantage. Popplewell J that this was just such a case – the defendant had sought to take "opportunistic and unreasonable advantage" of the claimant's mistake when it was obvious that an extension of time was appropriate. As a result, it was appropriate to award the claimant costs on the indemnity basis.

E -v- The Commissioners for Her Majesty's Revenue & Customs

We have devoted a separate chapter to litigants in person, but this case is also relevant to the issue of not taking a tactical advantage.

In this case, HMRC was criticised for failing to cooperate where they were up against a litigant in person with Asperger's syndrome.

The Appellant ("E") was issued with an excise duty assessment of £928 and a £185 fine having been found with 15kg of hand rolled tobacco in her possession at Dover docks. Her case was that she had been duped and used as a scapegoat.

The appellant was a "vulnerable adult". "This was apparent from the Notice of Appeal where the appellant stated that she suffered from

Asperger's Syndrome, Attention Deficit Hyperactivity Disorder (ADHD) and fibromyalgia".

The appellant appealed on the grounds of hardship. HMRC made a specific application to strike out the appeal on the grounds that E had failed to pursue the appeal properly.

> *"But beyond that is a more important point. The unspoken point being made here (which in other cases is spoken) is HMRC's belief that the BPP[3]sauce for their goose should in all cases, irrespective of the importance of the issue, be sauce for an appellant's gander. In other words they seem to be using any non-compliance with directions as a weapon with which to engineer a strike out. But why in this particular case? Both members of the panel here have been involved in many other cases involving litigants in person where HMRC do not seek to take any points about a failure to comply with directions and where the HMRC representative will go out of their way to help the appellant (thus furthering the overriding objective in Rule 2 of the FTT Rules and cooperating with the Tribunal).*
>
> *That it is not just HMRC who seek to use infringements of directions as a weapon can be seen from, among other cases, Essential Telecom Ltd v HMRC [2016] UKFTT 475 where the appellant sought to have HMRC debarred from the proceedings for being 24 hours late with a skeleton. There it was said:*
>
> *"22. We consider that there are two very relevant paragraphs in Denton which, in this case, we draw to the attention of the appellant:*
>
> *'40 Litigation cannot be conducted efficiently and at proportionate cost without (a) fostering a culture of compliance with rules, practice directions and court orders, and (b) cooperation between the parties and their lawyers. This applies as much to litigation undertaken by litigants in person as it does to others. This was part of the foundation of the Jackson report. Nor should it be overlooked that CPR rule 1.3 provides that "the parties are required to help the court to further the overriding objective". Parties who opportunistically and*

unreasonably oppose applications for relief from sanctions take up court time and act in breach of this obligation.

41 We think we should make it plain that it is wholly inappropriate for litigants or their lawyers to take advantage of mistakes made by opposing parties in the hope that relief from sanctions will be denied and that they will obtain a windfall strike out or other litigation advantage. In a case where (a) the failure can be seen to be neither serious nor significant, (b) where a good reason is demonstrated, or (c) where it is otherwise obvious that relief from sanctions is appropriate, parties should agree that relief from sanctions be granted without the need for further costs to be expended in satellite litigation. The parties should in any event be ready to agree limited but reasonable extensions of time up to 28 days as envisaged by the new rule 3.8(4).'

This approach has already been reflected in decisions of Tribunals. In Dorset Healthcare NHS Foundation Trust v MH [2009] UKUT 4 (AAC) the Administrative Appeals Chamber of the Upper Tribunal said of Rule 2 of the First-tier Tribunal Rules (Overriding Objective):

'Those provisions therefore impose an express obligation upon the parties to assist in the furtherance of the objective of dealing with cases fairly and justly, which includes the avoidance of unnecessary applications and unnecessary delay. That requires parties to cooperate and liaise with each other concerning procedural matters, with a view to agreeing a procedural course promptly where they are able to do so, before making any application to the tribunal. This is particularly to be expected where parties have legal representation.'"

"The Master correctly applied stages 1 and 2 of the three stages identified in the case of Denton v. White [2014] 1 WLR 3926. I raised with counsel the question of the applicability of the relief from sanctions criteria to late service of witness statements but having been taken to the Court of Appeal decision in the case of Chartwell Estate Agents Ltd v. Fergies Properties SA [2014] EWCA 506, I am sat-

> *isfied that the Denton criteria are properly to be applied. It is said that the Master failed to identify and evaluate all circumstances relevant to the overall justice of the case, i.e. the third and last of the Denton stages. I have already observed that in my view the Master was in this case very seriously hampered in his task by the fact that these applications came at the end of a busy day. He had just half an hour for hearing and deciding all three matters, any one of which could properly have taken half an hour or more on its own. Furthermore, no doubt to save time, the Claimant's counsel had made a number of concessions which would have appeared to cover all the important considerations for the purposes of the third Denton stage, in the process sidelining matters which, with the benefit of far more time at the hearing before me, I have been able to understand more fully. Looking at his judgment, the Master plainly did direct himself to the third of the Denton criteria, however, for the reasons I have already given and through no fault of the Master, the available time at the hearing did not allow for a full and detailed appreciation of all the matters relevant to that third consideration.*
>
> *I am accordingly going to allow this appeal"*

The Tribunal decided that the provisions impose an express obligation upon the parties to assist in the furtherance of the objective of dealing with cases fairly and justly, which includes the avoidance of unnecessary applications and unnecessary delay. That requires parties to cooperate and liaise with each other concerning procedural matters, with a view to agreeing a procedural course promptly where they are able to do so, before making any application to the tribunal and that "This is particularly to be expected where parties have legal representation."

> "*We rather incline to the view that if any party has failed to co-operate with the Tribunal in the manner described in Rule 8(3)(c) it is HMRC. They were the ones who should have (even if "must have" is going too far) realised the vulnerability of the appellant and should not only have made all appropriate adjustments themselves but should have informed the Tribunal, so that the rather unsuitable directions and letters from the Tribunal would not have been issued in*

the form they were and which could easily have led the panel hearing the application to take a very different course from the one it did. That would not have been just and fair."

This is another example of the Tribunal, in this instance, allowing relief in a case involving a litigant in person but also highlights the point about respondents not trying to take a tactical advantage out of the other party's failings or mistakes. Respondents have to tread a fine line as they must not be seen to take a tactical advantage but at the same time they need to act in the best interests of their clients.

14. Extending into other jurisdictions and general applicability to proceedings.

<u>William Martland v Revenue & Customs Commissioners (2018) [2018] UKUT 178 (TCC)</u>

It is clear from this case that the relief from sanctions principles are now being extended into wider areas, like a fast spreading virus.

In this tax appeal case it was found that the rule **applied to applications for permission to appeal to the First-tier Tribunal outside the relevant time limit.**

The appellant appealed against the First-tier Tribunal's decision to refuse his application to bring a late appeal against an assessment of excise duty and a penalty.

The tribunal had stated that, in considering the exercise of its jurisdiction to give permission for the late appeal, it was bound to apply the overriding objective set out in the Tribunal Procedure (First-tier Tribunal) (Tax Chamber) Rules 2009 r.2. It found that the 15-month delay in bringing the appeal was significant and serious. It held that the explanation given for the delay, namely the appellant's inability to afford representation, was not a reasonable excuse. It noted that the appellant could be made bankrupt if not permitted to appeal, but regarded that as a consequence of his failing to appeal in time.

It was held that Revenue and Customs Commissioners, Petitioners [2005] CSOH 135 ("Aberdeen") and Data Select Ltd v Revenue and Customs Commissioners [2012] UKUT 187 (TCC) provided lists of factors to be considered when considering whether to permit late tax or VAT appeals. The evolving approach to relief from sanctions under CPR r.3.9 and the changes made to that rule since Aberdeen and Data Select applied to applications for permission to appeal to the tribunal outside the relevant time limit.

The judge exercised discretion both under r.3.9 and regarding late appeals. The consequences of the judge's decision would often be the same in practical terms in both situations. In exercising judicial discretions generally, particular importance was to be given to the need for "litigation to be conducted efficiently and at proportionate cost", and "to enforce compliance with rules, practice directions and orders", as r.3.9 required. When considering whether to permit late appeals, the starting point was that permission should not be granted unless the tribunal was satisfied on balance that it should be. In considering that question, the tribunal could usefully follow the three-stage process set out in Denton v TH White Ltd [2014] EWCA Civ 906, Denton applied. On that approach, all the factors in Aberdeen and Data Select would be covered, without the need to refer back explicitly to those cases.

The Court asked whether the tribunal had wrongly taken the reason for the delay and the consequences of refusal of permission as a single question? All the relevant factors had to be weighed in the balance. The tribunal had considered the reason given for the delay and concluded that it did not amount to a reasonable excuse. It had then considered the consequences of refusing to extend time, and observed that they were a necessary consequence of a failure to appeal in time. The tribunal had considered the reason and the consequences separately and then included them both in its overall assessment. It had not erred in doing so.

Had the tribunal been wrong to find no sufficient reason to extend time in circumstances where the appellant considered that the relevant law was unsettled? The tribunal had considered the state of the case law and said that the appellant's case was neither very strong nor very weak and its strength should therefore have no weight for or against the extension of time. That had been a wholly reasonable approach. Where an appeal was hopeless in any event, it was not in the interests of justice to grant permission. Where an appeal had some merit, it was important that the tribunal at least considered the parties' arguments in outline. That was not in order to carry out a detailed evaluation of the case, but to form a general impression of its strength. In considering that point, the tribunal should not, absent exceptional circumstances, take into account evidence which was in dispute,. R. (on the application of Hysaj) v Secretary of State for the Home Department [2014] EWCA Civ 1633 was applied.

So, the Court also needs to take into account the overall merits of the appeal. It seems that the merits and strengths of the case are factors that play a key role in deciding whether all the circumstances of the case require relief to be granted. Put simply, the Court is more likely to grant relief in a strong case than one which has little merit. That is in line with the requirement to act justly and in the interests of the overriding objective. When making an application, therefore, it is worthwhile focusing on the prejudice to the client if the sanctions apply and highlighting the strengths of the case.

<u>Sabesan v London Borough of Waltham Forest [2018] EWHC 2373 (Admin)</u>

This judgment confirms that the Denton principles apply to an appeal from the Valuation Tribunal.

The proposed appellant was appealing against a decision of the Valuation Tribunal imposing council tax upon him. The appeal was filed five months late and the judge considered why the appeal was late and the principles to be applied.

The reasons for delay in filing the appeal were as follows:

i. He continued to pursue his claim for relief from his council tax liability through proceedings at the Thames Magistrates' Court.

ii. He was waiting for a reply from the Council to agree to extend time, so he made another application to the Magistrate's Court to set aside the liability orders made against him in respect of council tax. That application was heard on or about 13 February 2018. It was dismissed on the basis that he had waited too long to bring the action.

iii. He wrote to the High Court "a normal letter" about that time about the matter, "but they said they could not deal with the matter in a letter back to me".

iv. He attempted again to appeal the decision to impose council tax liability on him to the Thames Magistrates' Court, but another District Judge rejected the appeal.

v. He was unable to pay Counsel's fees.

The question arose as to what principles governed the judge's exercise of the discretion referred to regulation 43(2) of the 2009 Regulations, which provides that the appeal "may be dismissed if it is not made within four weeks"

The judge referred to the case of Paul Turner v South Cambridgeshire District Council [2016] EWHC 1017 (Admin) in which Mr Justice Warby was also considering an application for an extension of time to appeal under regulation 43 of the 2009 Regulations, which was two weeks late, and in which Warby J concluded at [7] that "[t]he Denton criteria are applicable [to such an application], either directly or by analogy". Having applied the Denton criteria, namely, the three stage process set out at [24] in the Denton case, Warby J concluded that the extension of time should not be granted.

Warby J said the following at [24] on the question of the principles that apply to an application for an extension of time under regulation 43 and the question of relief from sanctions:

> *"It is clear that Regulation 43 gives the Court a discretion to dismiss an appeal made out of time. The Regulation can be analysed as imposing a time limit which may be extended only if the court in its discretion agrees; or an automatic sanction from which relief must be sought; or as a ground on which the court may in its discretion dismiss an appeal. I do not believe it matters. The general rule is that appeal courts treat an application to extend time for appealing, when brought after the time limit has expired, as equivalent to an application for relief from sanctions from CPR 3.9; the court applies what have become known as the Mitchell/Denton principles. Sayers v Clarke Walker (A firm) [2002] EWCA Civ 645, [2002] 1 WLR 3095; R (Hysaj) v SSHD [2014] EWCA Civ 1633; [2015] 1 WLR 2472. It is common ground that in this case I should adopt that approach, and I agree that is appropriate."*

Counsel argued that the use of the words "may be dismissed" indicated that the time limit in regulation 43(2) is not an "absolute bar" and therefore there is no sanction in the 2009 Regulations for a late appeal to the High Court. It is not appropriate to take the Denton approach, which applies to an appeal brought under the CPR 52 in relation to an ordinary civil claim. Here is a separate statutory regime, in relation to which the wording of the regulation 43(2) indicates that a less stringent approach should be taken. The judge rejected that argument saying that:

> *"I can see no reason why a less rigorous approach should be taken. I do not consider that there is anything in the argument that the words "may be dismissed" used in regulation 43 of the 2009 Regulations, in contrast to the words "shall dismiss" used in regulation 21(2) coupled with a specific relief from sanction provision in regulation 21(6), indicate that a less stringent approach should be taken in relation to an application for an extension of time under regulation 43. It is appropriate that the 2009 Regulations, which are concerned with the*

appellate jurisdiction of the VTE, should have more detailed rules in relation to such appeals, while a reference to appeal to the High Court should recognise that the High Court retains discretion in relation to the granting of an extension of time. Nonetheless, that discretion must be exercised by reference to principle.

I believe that the correctness of the approach taken by Warby J in Turner as set out at [24] of his judgment in that case is reinforced by the general approach taken by the Court of Appeal to the question of compliance with procedural rules applicable to tribunals in BPP Holdings Ltd v Revenue and Customs Commissioners (Practice Note) [2016] EWCA Civ 121; [2016] 1 WLR 1915. In relation to an application for extension of time in the context of tribunal proceedings, Lord Justice Ryder in BPP Holdings case referred at [44] to the judgment of Mr Justice Morgan, sitting in the Upper Tribunal Tax and Chancery Chamber in the case of Data Select Limited v HMRC [2012] STC 2195, where Morgan J applied CPR 3.9 by analogy to the application for extension of time made by HMRC in that case. The Data Select case, of course, pre-dates the Denton and Hysaj cases, but it indicates a consistent approach."

The judge therefore applied the three stage process summarised at in the Denton case:

i. First stage – seriousness and significance of the failure to comply with the deadline: The appellant filed his appeal five months late. That is a serious and significant delay..

ii. Second stage – why the default occurred: none of the reasons advanced by the applicant in his witness statement came close to providing an acceptable reason for a failure to file within the deadline, much less a delay of five months in doing so. His financial difficulties are, of course, unfortunate and attract sympathy, but cannot of themselves excuse a delay of five months.

iii. Third stage – the need to evaluate "all of the circumstances of the case, so as to enable [the Court] to deal justly with the application, including factors (a) and (b) of Rule 3.9", which apply by analogy if not directly. Factors (a) and (b) of CPR 3.9 required the judge to have regard to the need for litigation to be conducted efficiently and at proportionate cost, and to consider the need to enforce compliance with rules, practice directions and orders. Counsel's submissions in relation to this third stage were that the applicant was not someone who was sitting on his hands or who had gone to sleep on his rights. As his witness statement makes clear, he was trying to assert his rights, but he was confused as to how to do so, and he had "become lost in the forest". Having regard to all the circumstances of the case, including the factors mentioned, the judge found that there was no basis on which he could justify granting an extension of time in this case.

Conclusion

So it can be seen from the above categories that Relief from sanctions is applicable to the litigation system from start to finish and is now being used in other jurisdictions such as tribunals. Defendants are now able to rely upon relief from sanctions in a wide variety of cases to deliver a knock out blow to opponents, which highlights the need to present any application for relief from sanction with great care and attention to detail.

CHAPTER NINE
LESSONS FROM CASE LAW

Delay in litigation is inevitable and raising arguments for or against relief from sanctions applications is now part and parcel of every litigator's repertoire.

What has been seen over the years is that the tougher approach to non-compliance with procedural orders heralded by Mitchell and then modified by Denton has become ingrained.

The Denton cases have introduced more flexibility into how the courts should approach applications for relief from sanctions. The third stage test of "all the circumstances" is a catch all allowing a judge to find a way to grant relief where justice demands it. The "buffer" provision allows the parties to agree extensions of 28 days where a hearing date is not affected.

However, the Court of Appeal is still sending out the message that courts are to take a strict approach to compliance. In light of this there is undoubtedly greater incentive on parties to avoid being in a situation where they have to seek relief.

It is clear from the decisions emanating from the Court of Appeal that the outcome of applications for relief can still be very unpredictable. The entire context of a claim will be considered and taken into account. This means on one day, before one judge, a one-day breach may be considered serious enough to justify no relief being granted and on another occasion before a different judge, a breach may be considered serious, but relief still be granted. Ultimately the discretion of the judge when applying the Denton test is extremely wide and the particular features a judge may consider important can vary considerably. This makes predicting the outcome of any application and preparing for one a difficult task.

There is one common theme which should be taken on board. The conduct of the parties before and after the actual breach is likely to play a considerable role in whether relief will be granted. Most important of all, if a breach is anticipated, steps should be taken to notify the Court and resolve the issue prior to the breach occurring. Similarly, as soon as it becomes apparent there has been a breach, an appropriate Application for relief should be issued. Any attempts to get around the breach are likely to be held against the defaulting party when it comes to applying the Denton Test.

The Denton principles have been held to apply even in areas of the law not governed by the CPR. For example, in BPP Holdings v Revenue And Customs [2016] EWCA Civ 121, the Court of Appeal had to consider conflicting Upper Tribunal decisions on whether the stricter approach to compliance with rules and directions made under the CPR applied to cases in the tax tribunals. The Senior President of Tribunals concluded that: "for the reasons I shall explain, I am of the firm view that the stricter approach is the right approach." Specialist courts and tribunals that do not apply the Denton approach are now the exception rather than the rule. It is a wonder why more litigants have not resorted to arbitration, in which parties can set their own pace to the proceedings.

From the start it was clear that there was a risk of confusion caused by lack of uniformity in the Courts' approach. Various steps were taken to try to combat this, ranging from judicial training to the designation of specialist Court of Appeal judges to sit in particular cases. It is hard to judge whether these efforts were successful but the continual flow of reported decisions would suggest that they were not wholly successful. The reality is that, even at Court of Appeal level, decisions are being reached that are difficult to reconcile with each other.

There is still a contradiction between, on the one hand, the desire to take a more robust approach to procedural non-compliance and, on the other, a recognition that that robust approach may operate harshly and unjustly against the incompetent party with a good case. Mitchell struck the balance firmly in favour of the former approach. Denton resulted in a softening of the hard operation of the rule, but inevitably the room for manoeuvre created by Denton was accompanied by more uncertainty of outcome. Denton may have resolved the law on breaches of rules and Court orders, but in relation to specific situations there has been an increase in uncertainty.

There is little consistency between decisions made by different judges. Unfortunately, the Jackson reforms were implemented at a time when there has been unprecedented pressure on the MOJ and Court resources, with budget cuts. The situation in many court centres remains difficult with staffing cuts, court closures and the disillusionment of experienced judges. Many Courts have closed, under the cloak of modernisation and the Reform Programme.

In November 2017, the Chancellor Philip Hammond reiterated that the Ministry of Justice will have to make £600m in savings by the end of the decade. The Treasury committed to reduce the department's spending from £6.6bn in 2017/18 to £6bn by 2019/20. Over the same period, spending on health, defence, the Home Office and education will all rise. HMCTS estimates it can reduce the number of cases held in physical courtrooms by 2.4m a year, enabling further attrition of the courts estate and cutting staff numbers by 40% to 10,000. I do foresee that when the online Court is introduced and digitisation spreads across the Court system, the majority of interlocutory applications such as for relief from sanction will take place online or by telephone.

One suspects that the online Court is more about cutting costs than increasing efficiency and assisting litigants to access the Courts. A two-tier judicial system has emerged with a rolls Royce Service and technological integration in the Rolls Building, the High Court, and some specialist tribunals, but a poorer service elsewhere. As a Deputy District Judge I have not received any training or feedback on relief from sanctions for years. No doubt in future this will be another function delegated to Legal advisers.

The question, which has not yet been addressed, is whether it is fair to apply the same approach to relief from sanctions in every Court and level of case. Having to vacate a trial date on a fast track case in Birkenhead where another date can easily be arranged is perhaps less serious than having to vacate a multi track trial in the High Court.

There is also a contradiction between the overriding objective for parties to co-operate and save Court resources and the limits imposed through relief applications on the parties' ability to vary directions or waive non-compliance. The result has inevitably been a proliferation of applications. Parties are not even apparently able to agree to an application for relief, so as to save Court time and costs.

Despite this, the best advice is to try and reach agreement unless you are confident that the other party will lose the application. Applications for relief have become a powerful weapon in the Litigation armoury although as with any skirmish, compromise is advisable to win the overall battle.

Conclusion

It can be seen from this Chapter that the rule on relief from sanction has extended its tentacles into almost every area of litigation and the principles always need to be considered when dealing with a situation where a deadline has been missed or a rule has been breached.

CHAPTER TEN
APPLICATIONS AND HOW TO WIN THEM

Applications for relief from sanction are common as problems with deadlines are a litigator's curse. No-one is perfect and every lawyer makes mistakes: Hence the requirement for professional indemnity insurance. Compliance with rules and directions have become a priority for the Courts and that is not likely to change. Complying with procedures is as important a part of the litigator's role as analysing and presenting the case. Hopefully this Guide will assist you in dealing with any application for relief from sanction that you encounter in practice.

2017 saw a number of decisions in which the English courts, both at first instance and on appeal, have re-emphasised the message that those who fail to comply with procedural rules should expect little sympathy, at least where they fail to take prompt steps to put matters right.

We have continued to see cases which illustrate that the courts remain willing to take tough decisions against those who flout the rules. The decisions outlined below are consistent with that trend, and arguably mark an increase in the frequency with which such decisions are being made in a wide variety of contexts. The obvious overall messages for litigating parties are:

- ensure compliance with rules and orders so far as possible;
- make an early application for more time where it appears a deadline cannot be met; and
- apply promptly for relief from any applicable sanction where things have gone wrong.

The case of *Griffith v Gourgey* [2017] EWCA Civ 926 acts as a reminder that parties will not be given a second bite at the cherry when it comes to relief from sanctions. The court cannot hear a second application for relief unless there has been a material change of circumstances since the first application was determined. That will be the case whether the first application was refused outright or was granted on conditions which have not been fulfilled.

It was recently decided in the case of *Broughal v Walsh Brothers Builders Ltd & Anor* [2018] EWCA Civ 1610 that there is no basis for arguing that a judge who refused an application for permission to appeal on the paper should not deal with the actual appeal relating to relief from sanctions. It was held that previous involvement in the appeal process does not, of itself, preclude a judge from hearing the appeal.

It is sometimes impossible to reach a compromise on directions timetables with other parties. That may be because other parties or their lawyers are actively trying to avoid doing what they have been ordered to do or to create a false sense of urgency and pressure by taking an aggressive approach to procedural or other issues. They may hope that by being intransigent, they can force your client to abandon their claim or defence and put them under pressure.

In any scenario, it is wise to proceed on the assumption that there will in due course be a contested application for relief from sanction, rather than in the hope that parties will suddenly see reason. Given the uncertainty Denton has created as to how applications will be resolved, such applications should always be taken seriously.

The best way of dealing with and winning any contested hearing, is clearly to identify the potential issue in advance and devise a strategy to make you look as good as possible when the matter goes before the judge. This does not mean simply complying with directions. At times it is obvious that compliance will be impossible, or that the other side will never accept that you have complied with directions. The question is how to deal with, explain and justify non-compliance. On the other hand, if you are the party trying to ensure compliance with orders, or have been affected by another party's delay, the question is how to prepare the ground for arguments that non-compliance has been serious and had a prejudicial impact on your case.

Each case turns on its own facts and so the authorities can only provide limited guidance as to whether relief is likely to be given in certain situations. The outcome will very much depend on the judge and where their sympathies are led. With hard work and preparation there is plenty of scope to turnaround a challenging situation.

Litigators know that things can go wrong. Planning for things to go wrong is not a sign of weakness or defeatism. All firms have systems in place to ensure that things go right and to diarise dates, but your contingency plan provides the essential safety net. Further effective contingency planning will feed back into the department and cut down on mistakes in the first place. Hopefully this Guide can form part of your contingency plan.

I have therefore set out some practical tips for when it comes to non-compliance with orders, rules and practice directions:

Pre-Breach

- Ensure that parties set a realistic timetable from the outset.
- Diarise dates for compliance (in particular costs budgets – see below)
- Anticipate non-compliance and, in good time, try and agree with your opponent a 'buffer order' to extend time using the provisions of CPR3.8(4).
- In the absence of agreement from your opponent, apply for an extension of time. But do make sure that applications are made at the earliest possible opportunity so that you avoid having to seek retrospective permission as this will be treated as an application for relief from sanctions.

- If you are having difficulties with a deadline or if there is any doubt over the wording of an order – communicate with the court at the earliest possible opportunity.

- Apply in advance. The hearing often takes a long time to be listed and may take place after the deadline, but as long as you applied in advance you should be ok.

- Do not assume the court shall approve a consent order where the parties have agreed an extension of time. Make sure you have obtained court approval before relying on any extension agreed between the parties.

Making an Application

Practitioners all work to avoid mistakes, and systems are in place, however problems can still occur. An awareness of the potential problems, risk management and an appreciation that mistakes can be made can serve to reduce the number of problems occurring.

Any application made should be perfect the forms accurately completed, witness statements clear, concise, detailed and well drafted and everything filed and served in good time.

The important thing is to be clear about the decisions you are making and, if relevant speak with your indemnity insurers.

If the position is hopeless then it is advisable to recognised this at the outset and mitigate the position as much as you can. Hopeless applications to the court will only increase costs.

Even if the position is hopeless there may be other escape routes. For example, the law relating to service of a claim form within the four month period is very strict. It will be rare for a court to grant an extension. However:-

- If the limitation period has not expired you can try issue again. (This May amount to an abuse of process). If this is the situation don't forget to mention to the Court about the resulting increase in costs and Court time that will be wasted.
- If the limitation period has expired, in personal injury cases, then you can make an application under Section 33.
- If the position cannot be salvaged then you must advise your client to take independent legal advice.

10 Top Tips

1. Ripeness is all

If you do miss a deadline, act promptly. Delays in seeking relief, especially when the non-compliance impacts on other aspect of the court's timetable, seems to be one of the most significant reasons for applications being refused.

Address mistakes, openly, honestly and promptly. Many mistakes can be rectified if dealt with early. The issue of delay in making an application is always a relevant factor. An application should be made within days, not weeks. It is always more impressive when the applicant has realised the mistake and then makes the application immediately.

2. Honesty is the Best Policy

Avoid the "cover-up" of the mistake which as in politics is almost always far more harmful than the mistake itself. The costs, expense and delay to the client are made much worse.

If you, or your firm, have made a mistake admit it. The fee earner responsible, or the head of department, should state clearly that they admit responsibility. In many cases this is obvious in any event, however most judges respond positively to admissions of responsibility. (subject to the views of your professional indemnity insurers). If it is the client's fault as they were unavailable or on holiday, give as reasonable and persuasive evidence as possible.

3. Rectify the Breach

Any default will look even worse if it is not corrected before the hearing. The fact that a party remains in default at the date of the hearing is likely to be a key, if not determinative, factor, as the Judge will think that the case is doomed to failure. This was demonstrated in the case of Sinclair v Dorset & Whitney in which the Judge commented:

> "*Further, even now, some eight weeks after the extended deadline, the claimants are still not offering security which is satisfactory.*"
> (Mr Justice Popplewell in Sinclair -v- Dorsey & Whitney [2015] EWHC 3888 (Comm).)

4. The Devil is in the Detail

Make sure evidence addresses the Denton principles and relief from sanction – a surprising number of applicants do not quote CPR Part 3.9!

The court needs to know how a party has got itself into the situation and is equally entitled to a detailed explanation. Give the court a clear and concise explanation and make it clear that this is an explanation and not an excuse. Sometimes there is insufficient detail to explain how an insurer failed to deal with an issue for example.

Make sure to include Denton principles in application to set aside judgment. Focus on the strong points – there is no point arguing there was a good reason for non-compliance if there was not. It is surprising how often an applicant does not quote the rule and deal with each aspect in turn. Counsel cannot give evidence. There is no point in arguing that a mistake by a solicitor owing to work pressures, illness or holiday commitments is good reason. The cat ate my homework was never a good excuse at school, let alone in practice!

Never make a half-hearted application to the Court assuming that, since this is only a trivial default, relief will be granted. This is a risky assumption. First, the judge may not share your assumption, secondly if you fail in your attempt this is, effectively, the end of the line and you are stuck with the same arguments on appeal.

On the other hand, it is important to strike a balance. Many witness statements in support of, and in opposition to, an application provide the court with extracts from the Court of Appeal judgments. Most judges are now familiar with the Denton principles. Arguing points of law in a witness statement add to the time and expense.

Keep the statement as short as possible, within reason. Set out the relevant background to the matter; explain why the breach occurred and what has been done to remedy the situation.

Don't forget to sign the application notice and statement and include a draft order with directions to trial, if possible, so the Court can see what direction the case is going if relief is granted.

5. Grasp the Nettle

When matters go wrong on a file it often becomes a cursed Problem File. It is often passed onto someone else. So the courts often see witness statements that say:

> *"I now have conduct of this matter because I am the newest/youngest/most senior person in the department and the fee earner left or everyone else realised that this file was a hospital pass."*

Even if the statement does not say that expressly, judges can recognise a "hospital pass" file. It is not difficult to read between the lines and Judges are often unimpressed. Any personal sympathy for the litigator involved is overtaken by anger with the firm that put the litigator in that situation. Judges also expect insurers to have procedures in place.

If a decision is made that problem files should be passed on they need to be moved to someone senior and with considerable experience, such as the head of Department or team. You may also need to notify your professional indemnity insurers.

Consider whether to adopt the "scapegoat" or "white knight" strategy, stressing how another fee earned was responsible and you have been handed a hospital pass but are determined to turn the case around. Focus on all the circumstances and the impact if relief is not granted, or that it will save time and expense if the case can be resurrected.

Alternatively take responsibility and adopt the "mea culpa" approach. Preferably attend the hearing rather than employing an advocate. The judge will be reluctant to disappoint the litigator in person if they are falling on their sword

Consider attending the hearing even if you are instructing an advocate. Sometimes matters come up at a hearing for relief from sanctions which require clarification.

Having the relevant person present, together with the file, can speed things up and be a great help. This helps both in relation to past conduct and also the proposed directions/future management of the case.

6. Attack is the Best Form of Defence

It is always advantageous to focus on the other party's failings and refusal to answer correspondence or to cooperate in accordance with the overriding objective.

Can the other party consent to an application? Best not to rely upon consent order and attend the hearing if in any doubt. Focus on the unreasonable conduct of the opponent and point to their own failings adopting the "log in your own eye" principle.

Argue that the other party are being unreasonable if they refuse to agree to the Court granting relief and if they argue that that they cannot agree as it is within the discretion of the Court which has to grant relief, argue that there was no reason for them to raise any objection even if the ultimate decision lies with the Court.

If the other party consents, but states that it is in the discretion of the Court, be prepared to argue that their attendance at the hearing was unnecessary. The Court may award you your costs or at least make a Costs in the case order.

7. All the circumstances

Consider falling back on the argument of "all the circumstances and the interests of justice." Is the client's recourse to a loss of chance negligence claim really going to result in the same compensation, or will they get less and incur further costs? Will it be possible to issue a new claim and if so will that result in further costs being incurred and wasted Court time?

8. Litigant in Person

If you are not legally represented, explain the circumstances and the limits of your understanding and unfamiliarity with the Court processes as the Court may be more sympathetic to you, particularly if you are up against an insurer or large business with deep pockets

9. Accurate Time Estimates

The applicant is expected to say how long the application will take to be heard. If application is going to be contested then the application is rarely going to be shorter than an hour. If the time estimate is 10 minutes and two advocates turn up then the case is likely to be adjourned and this will normally result in the responsible party paying the costs. It is unlikely that the Court will deal with such an application on the papers unless there is a supporting consent order.

If it is clear that the time estimate is inadequate then it is also the responsibility of the respondent to point this out to the applicant, and the court, at the earliest opportunity.

If the application is consented to then, again, the parties should let the court know at the earliest opportunity.

10. Plan of Action

CPR 3.9 and the Denton criteria arise in the context whereby judges are under a legal duty to manage cases in accordance with the overriding objective (CPR 1.2 & 1.4) and the parties are required to help the court to further the overriding objective (1.3). It can assist you if you include including draft directions which put will put the case back on track.

Defending an Application

Here are some top tips if the shoe is on the other foot.

The first thing to appreciate is that you are not actually "defending" or trying to exploit the other party's errors or omissions even if you actually are! You are just trying to assist the Court by pointing out how egregious the other party's delays have been and how badly this has impacted on your client.

If you find yourself in a position where your opponent requires relief from sanctions do not view it as an opportunity to gain a tactical advantage but co-operate as in the Denton cases the Court of Appeal warned that parties who unreasonably oppose applications for relief (and time extensions) will be penalised. – we do see many respondents trying to dress up tactical advantage as being helpful to the Court – is it necessary for the respondent to attend the hearing if they do not object?

If the other party's case has been struck out remind the Court that the client can always make a professional negligence claim.

If the applicant is a litigant in person be prepared for the Court to allow more leeway than usual.

Appealing

If you lose at the application, consider appealing. You should ask for permission to appeal at the first hearing. However, remember the limitations and difficulties such as the Court's reluctance to interfere with case management decisions or to encourage satellite litigation. Remember there are only 14 days to file an appeal.

If you are going to appeal it is important to follow the rules carefully, file and serve the right documents within time, give proper grounds of appeal and file a proper skeleton argument.

Going Forward

If you win you cannot afford to sit back and relax. You don't want to be in the same position again as it will be even more difficult to obtain relief. Consider which fee earner should deal with the matter in the future. If relief from sanctions is granted then get on with the case with speed and diligence. In no circumstances allow any further breaches to occur. Where there is a second application for relief from sanctions, the case does not normally go in favour of the applicant.

Whoever deals with the matter should explain the situation to the client and make sure that the case stays on track going forwards.

However tempting it may be to put a stressful experience behind you, those incidents that lead to the need for relief from sanctions are often warning signs that issues need to be addressed. Even if relief is granted in a particular case the experience can be used to ensure that it does not happen again. Clearly, it is a good idea from a risk management point of view to ensure that the same problem does not arise again. Systems can be introduced or strengthened, a litigator's workload may be an issue that needs addressing or re training may be required.

Conclusion

We would also recommend distributing this guide to all fee earners so that they have some assistance in dealing with these applications, which unfortunately often arise in practice.

For specific advice on a particular case, for representation at a hearing or to report an interesting decision, please do not hesitate to get in touch.

MORE BOOKS BY LAW BRIEF PUBLISHING

A selection of our other titles available now:-

'In My Backyard! A Practical Guide to Neighbourhood Plans' by Dr Sue Chadwick
'A Practical Guide to the Law Relating to Food' by Ian Thomas
'A Practical Guide to the Ending of Assured Shorthold Tenancies' by Elizabeth Dwomoh
'Commercial Mediation – A Practical Guide' by Nick Carr
'A Practical Guide to Financial Services Claims' by Chris Hegarty
'The Law of Houses in Multiple Occupation: A Practical Guide to HMO Proceedings' by Julian Hunt
'A Practical Guide to Unlawful Eviction and Harassment' by Stephanie Lovegrove
'A Practical Guide to Solicitor and Client Costs' by Robin Dunne
'Artificial Intelligence – The Practical Legal Issues' by John Buyers
'A Practical Guide to Wrongful Conception, Wrongful Birth and Wrongful Life Claims' by Rebecca Greenstreet
'Occupiers, Highways and Defective Premises Claims: A Practical Guide Post-Jackson – 2nd Edition' by Andrew Mckie
'A Practical Guide to Financial Ombudsman Service Claims' by Adam Temple & Robert Scrivenor
'A Practical Guide to the Law of Enfranchisement and Lease Extension' by Paul Sams
'A Practical Guide to Marketing for Lawyers – 2nd Edition' by Catherine Bailey & Jennet Ingram
'A Practical Guide to Advising Schools on Employment Law' by Jonathan Holden
'Certificates of Lawful Use and Development: A Guide to Making and Determining Applications' by Bob Mc Geady & Meyric Lewis
'A Practical Guide to the Law of Dilapidations' by Mark Shelton

'A Practical Guide to the 2018 Jackson Personal Injury and Costs Reforms' by Andrew Mckie
'A Guide to Consent in Clinical Negligence Post-Montgomery' by Lauren Sutherland QC
'A Practical Guide to Running Housing Disrepair and Cavity Wall Claims: 2nd Edition' by Andrew Mckie & Ian Skeate
'A Practical Guide to the General Data Protection Regulation (GDPR)' by Keith Markham
'A Practical Guide to Digital and Social Media Law for Lawyers' by Sherree Westell
'A Practical Guide to Holiday Sickness Claims – 2nd Edition' by Andrew Mckie & Ian Skeate
'A Practical Guide to Inheritance Act Claims by Adult Children Post-Ilott v Blue Cross' by Sheila Hamilton Macdonald
'A Practical Guide to Elderly Law' by Justin Patten
'Arguments and Tactics for Personal Injury and Clinical Negligence Claims' by Dorian Williams
'A Practical Guide to QOCS and Fundamental Dishonesty' by James Bentley
'A Practical Guide to Drone Law' by Rufus Ballaster, Andrew Firman, Eleanor Clot
'Practical Mediation: A Guide for Mediators, Advocates, Advisers, Lawyers, and Students in Civil, Commercial, Business, Property, Workplace, and Employment Cases' by Jonathan Dingle with John Sephton
'Practical Horse Law: A Guide for Owners and Riders' by Brenda Gilligan
'A Comparative Guide to Standard Form Construction and Engineering Contracts' by Jon Close
'A Practical Guide to Compliance for Personal Injury Firms Working With Claims Management Companies' by Paul Bennett
'A Practical Guide to the Landlord and Tenant Act 1954: Commercial Tenancies' by Richard Hayes & David Sawtell
'A Practical Guide to Personal Injury Claims Involving Animals' by Jonathan Hand
'A Practical Guide to Psychiatric Claims in Personal Injury' by Liam Ryan
'Introduction to the Law of Community Care in England and Wales' by Alan Robinson
'A Practical Guide to Dog Law for Owners and Others' by Andrea Pitt

'Ellis and Kevan on Credit Hire – 5th Edition' by Aidan Ellis & Tim Kevan
'RTA Allegations of Fraud in a Post-Jackson Era: The Handbook – 2nd Edition' by Andrew Mckie
'RTA Personal Injury Claims: A Practical Guide Post-Jackson' by Andrew Mckie
'On Experts: CPR35 for Lawyers and Experts' by David Boyle
'An Introduction to Personal Injury Law' by David Boyle
'A Practical Guide to Claims Arising From Accidents Abroad and Travel Claims' by Andrew Mckie & Ian Skeate
'A Practical Guide to Cosmetic Surgery Claims' by Dr Victoria Handley
'A Practical Guide to Chronic Pain Claims' by Pankaj Madan
'A Practical Guide to Claims Arising from Fatal Accidents' by James Patience
'A Practical Approach to Clinical Negligence Post-Jackson' by Geoffrey Simpson-Scott
'A Practical Guide to Personal Injury Trusts' by Alan Robinson
'Employers' Liability Claims: A Practical Guide Post-Jackson' by Andrew Mckie
'A Practical Guide to Subtle Brain Injury Claims' by Pankaj Madan
'The Law of Driverless Cars: An Introduction' by Alex Glassbrook
'A Practical Guide to Costs in Personal Injury Cases' by Matthew Hoe
'A Practical Guide to Alternative Dispute Resolution in Personal Injury Claims – Getting the Most Out of ADR Post-Jackson' by Peter Causton, Nichola Evans, James Arrowsmith
'A Practical Guide to Personal Injuries in Sport' by Adam Walker & Patricia Leonard
'The No Nonsense Solicitors' Practice: A Guide To Running Your Firm' by Bettina Brueggemann
'Baby Steps: A Guide to Maternity Leave and Maternity Pay' by Leah Waller
'The Queen's Counsel Lawyer's Omnibus: 20 Years of Cartoons from The Times 1993-2013' by Alex Steuart Williams

These books and more are available to order online direct from the publisher at www.lawbriefpublishing.com, where you can also read free sample chapters. For any queries, contact us on 0844 587 2383 or mail@lawbriefpublishing.com.

Our books are also usually in stock at www.amazon.co.uk with free next day delivery for Prime members, and at good legal bookshops such as Hammicks and Wildy & Sons.

We are regularly launching new books in our series of practical day-to-day practitioners' guides. Visit our website and join our free newsletter to be kept informed and to receive special offers, free chapters, etc.

You can also follow us on Twitter at www.twitter.com/lawbriefpub.

www.ingramcontent.com/pod-product-compliance
Lightning Source LLC
LaVergne TN
LVHW052326200926
848481LV00002B/679
9781911035442

Peter Causton is a practising solicitor and barrister at Whitestone Chambers, a Civil and Commercial mediator and Deputy District Judge. He has set up ProMediate (UK) Limited which is a registered Civil Mediation Council Mediation Provider.